Praise for M

"Wonderfully written with n[...] treasure inside your dreams, Linda Schiller's new book will bring you home to the beating heart of your inner wisdom."
—Robert Waggoner, author of
Lucid Dreaming: Gateway to the Inner Self

"Rarely do we find a writer like Linda who makes the subject of dreams both accessible for novices and enriching for experts. She opened my eyes to new avenues for dream exploration and interpretation, and that's saying something considering that I've studied the subject from all angles during the past twenty-five years!"
—J.M. DeBord, author of
The Dream Interpretation Dictionary

"A brilliant look at the role of dreams in our everyday lives and how dreams can be used to inform healing, creativity, and spiritual growth. Helping professionals seeking a way to aid clients through dream work will undoubtedly benefit from the many examples presented here. The general reader will find a path to deeper understanding of personal consciousness."
—Jean Campbell, editor of *DreamTime*
and author of *Group Dreaming*

"In *Modern Dreamwork*, Linda Yael Schiller takes us on a scintillating trip into the luminous and deep world of dreams and shows us how to 'dream ourselves home' to the hidden core of our being. Weaving together the bright threads of dreams, myths, archetypes, and stories, *Modern Dreamwork* illuminates ways of accessing the spiritual wisdom of our night-time dreams."
—Dr. Clare Johnson, author of
Llewellyn's Complete Book of Lucid Dreaming

Modern
DREAMWORK

About the Author

Linda Yael Schiller, MSW, LICSW, is a body, mind, and spiritual psychotherapist, consultant, author, and international speaker. She has taught dreamwork and run dream groups for over thirty years. Trained in a number of integrated trauma treatment modalities, she teaches and consults on trauma treatment, PTSD, and nightmares. Linda developed and authored original theory on relational group work while a professor at Boston University, and has published numerous articles, audio programs and poetry. She is a dancer, a student of Kabbalah, and loves historical novels and science fantasy. Born in Buffalo, New York, she lived in Israel for five years and then moved to Boston, MA, where she currently resides with her husband, daughter, and two cats. She loves to spend time outdoors hiking, gardening, and swimming. Visit her at www.lindayaelschiller.com or www.moderndreamwork.com.

Modern
DREAMWORK

New Tools for Decoding
Your Soul's Wisdom

LINDA YAEL SCHILLER

LLEWELLYN PUBLICATIONS
WOODBURY, MINNESOTA

FIRST EDITION
First Printing, 2019

Book design: Samantha Penn
Cover design: Kevin Brown
Editing: Annie Burdick

Llewellyn Publications is a registered trademark of Llewellyn Worldwide Ltd.

Library of Congress Cataloging-in-Publication Data
Names: Yael Schiller, Linda, author.
Title: Modern dreamwork : new tools for decoding your soul's wisdom / Linda
  Yael Schiller.
Description: Woodbury, Minnesota : LLewellyn Publications, 2020. | Includes
  bibliographical references.
Identifiers: LCCN 2019040249 (print) | LCCN 2019040250 (ebook) | ISBN
  9780738761824 (paperback) | ISBN 9780738762074 (ebook) | ISBN
  9780738762074 (ebook)
Subjects: LCSH: Dreams.
Classification: LCC BF1078 .Y34 2020 (print) | LCC BF1078 (ebook) | DDC
  154.6/3—dc23
LC record available at https://lccn.loc.gov/2019040249
LC ebook record available at https://lccn.loc.gov/2019040250

Llewellyn Publications
A Division of Llewellyn Worldwide Ltd.
2143 Wooddale Drive
Woodbury, MN 55125-2989
www.llewellyn.com
Printed in the United States of America

Other Books by Linda Yael Schiller

Integrated and Comprehensive Treatment of Trauma

CONTENTS

ACKNOWLEDGMENTS

This book would not exist without the wisdom and support of my fellow dreamers and their kind and generous permission to share their dream travels. First to my own long-term dream circle of over thirty years: Lisa Kennedy, Marcia Lewin-Berlin, and Suzie Abu-Jabar. You cheered me on and encouraged me and held the vision even before I started the blog—telling me that I didn't have to wait until I had enough time to write a whole book, just start writing short bits now. I took your advice, and seven years later, here we are. Thank you for letting me interview you on your own visitation dreams. You are all such a gift in my life.

Thank you to my Thursday dream group: Joy Weider, Joyce Rosen, Marcia Post, Mia Woodford, Starr Potts, and Ruth Silverstein for your support, caring, and willingness to share your dreams with me, with each other, and now with the broader world. Special thanks to this crew for helping me come up with the acronym "GAIA." Thank you to all my clients who gave me permission to share their dream journeys in the service of helping others on their healing paths.

To my other dear friends for their unending enthusiasm, support, and offers of help: Julie Leavitt, dream-dancer and spirit-sister who helps me to embody my dreams; Diane Pardes, sister from another mother who has been traveling with me in this life longer than anyone except my parents and siblings; Sara Kopf Levine, woodswalker and ritual-builder who holds and offers the space; Beth Rontal, dear friend and colleague who has joined me on several dream adventures; Lynn Roberson, friend, healer, and Reiki master; Allison Rimm, my hero for getting out a book; Ellen Alfaro, adventure-sharer par excellance; and all my Torah Women and co-seekers. Thank you to David Kahn: friend, dreamer, and dancer who consulted with me on the neuroscience of dreams. Any inadvertent mistakes are mine.

It takes a village to write a book, and I have had wonderful editorial help along the way. First, an enormous thank-you to dreamworker, author, and editor par excellence Jason DeBord, who taught me how to go from "long-form writing 101" to "graduate school." Your generosity is unparalleled, and I have started a file of your writing tips! Amy Glaser at Llewellyn Worldwide has been such a source of support, encouragement, and great collaboration. Thank you also goes to the other wonderful staff at Llewellyn: cover artist Kevin Brown, who delighted my senses; editor Annie Burdick, whose careful reading made this manuscript better; Sami Sherratt; and Kat Sanborn. Many thanks for earlier editorial help to Melanie Gorman and Estella Arias, and to the web of support and dream connections that stretches from Jean Campbell, Dreamtime editor at IASD and to Lisa Hagen at Lisa Hagen Books. Thank you to fellow dream sister Lauren Schneider who helped me vision this through her Taropy reading. A big shout out to IASD—the International Association for the Study of Dreams. This welcoming worldwide organization supports and encourages dreamers, dream artists, dream scientists, and dream therapists, and has provided me with an international community of dreamers.

This book would not be here if not for the love, support, and inspiration of my daughter and husband. Sara, dreaming you home started this journey to take dreams out from the privacy of my own bed and head into the world—thank you so much for granting me the privilege of sharing your beginnings story. Steve, as always, you have been my rock, tending the home fires while I disappeared into writing or editorial land. Thank you both for giving me the time and space to birth this book.

INTRODUCTION

"One of the great gifts of darkness and the
night is our capacity to dream."
Estelle Frankel

Twenty years ago I dreamed my daughter home.

My husband and I were in the process of adopting from China. One day the agency director, Lillian, informed us that a baby girl had been found. She was about nine months old and we would be departing in three months to get her, making her a year old by the time she'd be ours. We were thrilled and a little anxious; we'd been hoping that the baby chosen for us would be younger so she would have spent less time in an orphanage.

Lillian said, "If this isn't the right baby for you, we can give you a different referral. It will take another few months."

What a decision! We'd already been waiting, hoping, and praying for more than a year since connecting with the agency. After a quick exchange of looks with my husband, I asked, "Can I go home and dream on it tonight?" Lillian agreed. She asked us to give her our decision by the next day.

That night I wrote in my dream journal, seeking help with this decision. I needed the answer to come through clearly, quickly, and unambiguously. My question: "Is this baby our daughter?" I think I even added, "I need a clear, definitive answer." Dreams can be so laden with symbols and metaphors—I didn't have the time to work on decoding it. We had to give our decision about adoption the next day. With so much at stake, I was quite bossy with my dream guide that night.

A little background information, known as *contextualizing* the dream, is needed for you to understand the guiding dream I received that night. Dreams are always sourced in the dreamer's personal life and therefore need to be understood in context. For our wedding anniversary earlier that year, my mother-in-law had gifted us a shed to store our gardening tools in, along with the labor of a contractor to build and install it. The most logical spot for the shed was underneath our high deck. As he began to install it, the contractor discovered that it was a little too big and wouldn't quite fit in that spot. But he said to us, "No problem, I can just dig down, lay a foundation, and it will fit just fine." Problem solved.

With that context as background, here is the dream I received that night: We were putting in a tool shed and it was a little bigger than we expected, but it fit fine.

The answer couldn't be clearer for me than that! We flew to China three months later and brought home our daughter. Our "just a little bigger than expected" baby is now twenty-two years old. We dug down and created a good foundation for her, using the "tools" we have as parents, and couldn't be more delighted with her and the choice my dream confirmed for us.

I dreamed her home.

Personal Dream Journey

That dream is one of many I've had that let me peek around the corners of time and space and pointed me toward new directions in my life. However, it was not until I began to track them and really pay attention to them as an adult that I began to appreciate the power of dreaming.

In my early twenties, a dream pointed me toward living in Israel for five years. While living there, I began to dream as well as speak in Hebrew (a hallmark of learning a language that I am still embarrassingly proud of, and which will become more relevant later on when we address the significance of what language we dream in). Upon returning to the US, I settled in Boston, just far enough away from my hometown of Buffalo, New York, but not the other side of the world anymore. A few years later, my friend Eve moved to town and invited me to join a dream-sharing group (aka a "dream circle") she was setting up. "I don't miss a thing about living in New York except my dream circle," she told me, "so I decided when I moved to Boston to set one up here."

The rest, as they say, is history. That dream circle continues thirty years later, even though by now Eve herself has moved on to sunnier climes. We stabilized with our current four members about twenty-five years ago. Initially we taught ourselves dream-work by reading books and attending workshops, and eventually we graduated to presenting a workshop together on the topic of how we created and maintained our long-term circle. We became a support system for each other, not only in our dream-work, but in our lives as well. By now we've shared births, deaths, weddings, bat mitzvahs, surgeries, conferences, and dancing, as well as dreams. The deep threads of the dreamwork have bound our lives together. Every time we feel particularly challenged to continue, and assess if we are able to, we discover new ways to make it work. We created a home base with each other, through the dream world. This possibility of finding home in the deepest sense of the word, through dreamwork and the personal ties created by dream-sharing, is available to all of us, and propels the arc of this book.

In addition to this personal resource, I find dreamwork invaluable in my professional life. As a psychotherapist, it is a large part of my repertoire in counseling clients. I have facilitated a professional dream circle that has also been ongoing for more than twenty years, and have been sharing the dreamwork skills and ideas described in this book to audiences around the country and the world for more than two decades.

The concepts of "home" and of "journey" infuse this book. Home is more than a physical locale; it involves a quest for meaning in our lives and a sense of belonging, and is often found inside oneself, not outside. The sanctuary inside of your own heart is where you can take refuge from the outside world. It is always available. *The Wizard of Oz* has always been one of my favorite touchstone stories about home and journeys of the mind, heart, and spirit. Dorothy returns home to Kansas after her journey through Oz.

Like Dorothy, your own journey through the magical land of dreams will lead you to unexpected places and surprising encounters. And like Dorothy, you too will find that the home you seek was available to you all along, perhaps buried just under the surface in your dreams. Let's turn now to *The Wizard of Oz* to explore its relevance to dreaming and how it can guide all of us on our journeys to the homes within ourselves.

Joining Dorothy on the Journey Home

"Just close your eyes, dear, click your heels together three times, and repeat, 'There's no place like home, there's no place like home, there's no place like home.'"

Most of us know this incantation. At the very end of her dreamlike journey through Oz, Dorothy receives the magic formula to return home from Glinda the Good Witch of the North. That had been Dorothy's goal the whole time she was in Oz: to find her way back home. All that remained to do was close her eyes, click the heels of her ruby slippers together three times, and say the words, "There's no place like home."

Working with our dreams can bring us back home to our most authentic selves. The goal of this book is to help you gain the skills to journey through the layers of your dreams, find what is hidden underneath the surface, and use this information to come home to the center of your own life. Dorothy has to travel through her own Oz-dream, including its nightmarish parts, to find her guides and companions and gain the wisdom and power she needs before she is given the gift of this ritual and incantation to get back home. When Scarecrow asks Glinda why she didn't just tell Dorothy how to do that when she first arrived in Oz, Glinda replies: "She wouldn't have believed me. She had to learn it for herself."

That message for Dorothy, and for us, is to learn firsthand for ourselves how to find our way back home. No one else can really tell us what our dreams mean. We must find that personal "aha!" moment of knowing for ourselves. Other people can help us on this journey, but the final arbitrator of the meaning of the dream is the dreamer.

All of us can get blown off course in our lives just as Dorothy did, and find ourselves in a very different landscape than the one we expected. Like Dorothy, we can become lost and disoriented; we can feel lonely, unwanted, frightened, or confused in our lives. We can find ourselves at crossroads, wondering, "Which way should I go now?"

We all need guidance at times. We need it when we have an important or difficult life decision to figure out (such as I did with my daughter), are stuck in a creative block, or are struggling with a personal or professional dilemma. We may also need it for resolving a traumatic event or deep loss, a worrisome health issue, a question about our path in life, or a desire to connect with a meaningful spirituality. Our dreams can connect us with the hidden core of our own truth in all these quests.

Simply stated, any question such as, "What would help me with this problem?" or "Which way should I go now in my life?" can be answered by our dreams. Mulder and Scully, the fictional FBI agents in the *X-Files,* told us that "dreams are answers to questions we haven't yet figured out how to ask." Unasked questions and answers show up in our dreams, too. Attending to our dreams gives us access to our deepest personal wisdom and an internal GPS to answer our own questions. The wayfaring system of our dreams can lead us home.

Our dreams are *alive.* These portals into our unconscious can feel as real as waking life. They are seeds that contain the potentiality for the whole, embodying our hopes, our fears, and our creativity. They serve as a permanent witness to our life's journeys, and are a portable, practical, and unlimited resource. This book invites you on a psycho-spiritual journey through the landscape of your dreams back to the home of your soul.

My orientation to dreamwork is an "Integrated Embodied Approach" based on the works of Carl Jung, Eugene Gendlin (author of the classic book on felt sense, *Focusing*), Joseph Campbell, and a plethora of spiritual teachers versed in Kabbalah, shamanic studies, and the mystic wisdom of many cultures. Principles from energy psychology and narrative therapy round out my clinical work and infuse this book as well. We will explore many dreamwork approaches and traditions, some as old as our caveman ancestors, some as new as neuroscience and quantum physics.

As anyone who has ever remembered a vivid dream knows, we do not just *have* a dream, we *experience* a dream. In "The Dream That Must Be Interpreted," from *The Essential Rumi*, the poet Rumi tells us, "Though we seem to be sleeping, there is an inner wakefulness that directs the dream, and that will eventually startle us back to the truth of who we are." In a dream we can simultaneously access multiple perspectives. We can be a character in our dream as well as an observer from the outside. We are as alive inside the dream as we are outside of it, and our night landscapes are often as real and as rich as our dayscapes. Dorothy knew this truth and tried to explain it to her friends when she woke up back home in Kansas at the end of the story. Although her Auntie Em and Uncle Henry and her friends tried to convince her that it was "just a dream", Dorothy insisted that it was a "very real place" and would not retreat from her belief. She went on to tell them about the places in Oz that she visited; some scary, but mostly beautiful.

As we journey through our dreams in this book, Dorothy's wisdom will be confirmed. We'll find that we are indeed in a "place" inside our dreams. Our dream landscapes can be beautiful, curious, and exciting; they can also be dark, dangerous, and frightening. Some are quickly forgotten. Others command our attention not only when we first awake, but all through the day and even weeks, months, and years later. One of my clients described this sensation as her "dream hangover." Many of us can still recall dreams we had in childhood. Some of us have repetitive dreams that loop and loop.

When repetitive dreams are frightening, they compel us with even more urgency to answer the ubiquitous questions: "What do these dreams mean, and why do I keep having them?" Recurring dreams are often a type of SOS from your unconscious; they urge you to take notice of something that needs your attention. Some recurring dreams become nightmares, which are pleas from the deep inner self to give your attention to something particularly urgent. In this book we will attend to these recurring missives from our soul-selves. Dreams contain messages for our lives. Some of these messages may be small ones, but others may be among the most important we ever receive, such as my dream that provided the final confirmation to adopt my daughter.

Our dreams are multi-layered like a pentimento—a fine-art term for a painting with another one painted right over it. Both paintings can occasionally be seen at the same time, as one layer ghosts through another. More often than not, though, the top layer must be carefully scraped back to reveal the second one underneath. Our dreams are like this—they come to us with multiple layers of meaning. We will learn to peel back these layers to get to the core of truth embedded within.

Guiding Philosophies

This book guides you in exploring your own dreams using three unique methods:

1. The "**Integrated Embodied Approach**" represents my overarching philosophy of working with dreams. I have honed this approach over more than thirty years of dreamwork. It incorporates into the dream exploration our physical awareness and body senses, our cognitions, the images themselves, our associations, our emotions and feelings, and our spiritual connections. In other words, it is a body/mind/spirit approach to dreams that gains our deepest and fullest understanding of these nocturnal messages. There are other dreamworkers who use embodied methods (Robert Bosnak is one who invites us to dive deeply and listen to our body), and other therapeutic practitioners who add dreamwork to their body-oriented treatments, such as Arnold Mindell and Eugene Gendlin. However, my integrated embodied approach to dreams attends to the uniqueness of each person and their dream life by offering the dreamer many modalities of working on a dream. I don't espouse a single orientation, such as that of Freud or Jung or Gestalt; rather I prefer a combination style of work, like an old Chinese menu: "One from column A and two from column B."

In doing so, I provide a way to honor our different needs and styles. Each dream gives up its secrets in different ways, so I believe that it is important to have a whole repertoire of options for interpreting dreams. Therefore, we also examine the imagery, metaphor, character, and story in our dreams, and explore our dreams from a shamanic perspective that recognizes forms of dreaming while awake as well as when asleep. Chapter 4 is your guide for "dreaming while awake."

My own professional background shares this integrative principle. Training in trauma treatment, neuroscience, energy psychology, body-oriented psychotherapies, and mindfulness meditation augment my clinical social work degree. Kabbalah, plus shamanic and religious studies, round out my knowledge base. I believe that we are beings made of both cells and of stardust, and I want to be able to offer my clients and students access to both realms, as well as to traditional evidence-based clinical approaches.

2. **The "PARDES" method:** The word *pardes* means "orchard" in Hebrew. It is also an acronym and a Kabbalistic approach to understanding the multiple layers of meaning in the Torah, the holy book in Judaism. I have applied this structure to understand and explore the multiple layers of our dreams. Chapter 5 covers this method and how I formulated it.

3. **The "GAIA" Method, or "the Guided Active Imagination Approach,"** is based on Carl Jung's work. Particularly useful with nightmares, I developed this method of dreamwork to provide a scaffolding to support us safely through the dark woods of our frightening dreams so we do not get triggered or overwhelmed when working with them. Chapter 11 on nightmares covers this method.

The language of dreams is not only highly symbolic, but also a great punster. For example, my client Marilyn describes a dream where she is walking in the woods and comes across a set of silverware—a spoon, a knife, and two forks (a salad fork and a dinner fork). She wonders what they are doing there.

During exploration of the dream, Marilyn gets the pun and realizes that she has been contemplating several "forks in the road," both in her personal and professional life. For me, this is one of the most enjoyable parts of dreamwork—finding those groan-producing puns and being thrilled by the creative ways our dreaming minds provide metaphor and magic.

What to Expect

Following a general orientation to the world of dreams in chapter 1, you will learn how to enhance your ability to remember them in chapter 2. Next, a detailed outline of dream *incubation* (dreaming "on purpose," to answer a question in your life, like I did with my daughter) is provided in chapter 3. Chapter 4 looks at sleeping and waking dreams with their companion states of synchronicity and intuition. The Kabbalah-based PARDES method of understanding the meaning of the layers of a dream follows in chapter 5, and our dream landscape is covered in chapter 6.

In subsequent chapters we delve into the all-important aspect of imagery in dreams, and how to use our dreams to enhance creativity and healing. People and animals are frequent visitors in our dreams; we will explore their messages, including the shamanic perspective of totem animals and spirit visits from departed loved ones. The final two chapters provide a plethora of dream discovery methods. They contain tools for examining the meanings of our dreams and our nightmares, and how to safely and creatively work with them. Through the GAIA method, you will learn how to contain, soothe, and transform your nightmares.

You can use this book as a roadmap to work with your dreams in a chapter-by-chapter sequence. Each chapter provides the building blocks for the ideas covered in the next one. By following this "yellow brick road" you will have a clear guide through which you can understand your dreams. Another equally valid way to use this book is as a topic-specific reference tool. If you have an explicit question about your dream, you can simply turn to the chapter that best addresses that question. Either way, by the end of this book, you will have skills and tools from multiple perspectives you can use as you embark on your dream journey.

Author and spiritual teacher Thomas Moore, author of *Care of the Soul*, speaks about dreams as home. Moore received a PhD in religious studies and became a psychotherapist following over a decade as a Catholic priest. He makes this connection between dreams and home in an interview with Oprah Winfrey on her podcast *Super Soul Sunday*:

"Your spiritual self was born in a dream, and when you dream, you are returning home. Your natural self is at home in the land where everything is both a physical fact and a poetic metaphor. When you dream, you are returning to the home, the very womb of your spirit and a world that speaks the language of your soul." Later he explains: it is like "we live our awake life at a top layer, and underneath you have this whole dream world with all of its meaning and suggestion and mystery."

Moore reminds us of the common phenomenon that we can both be in the dream and watching the dream simultaneously. It feels like a movie yet not quite, since we are often in it too. When asked if he was implying that our dream life is as real as our actual life, his response was, "Maybe more. Maybe more real."

EXERCISE

In preparation for your journey, I suggest purchasing a dream journal. It can be a simple spiral notebook or a beautiful bound art book. Take some time to decide which will inspire you the most to actually take on the discipline and practice of recording your dreams. Keep it right next to your bed at night, along with writing tools. Begin the practice of writing them down in your journal; along with the date you have them. If there are dreams from the past that have stayed with you, write these down as well, perhaps in a special section. As best as you can remember, date these previous dreams too. Long-remembered dreams from the past often still have a particular meaning and resonance for us. Additionally, you might like to think about whether there is anyone else in your life you would like to dream share with. Invite them to begin this dream-catching process as well.

One
....

ORIENTING TO THE WORLD OF DREAMS

"Dreams are illustrations ... from the book
your soul is writing about you."
Marsha Norman

A great many of us share memories and associations with *The Wizard of Oz*. It is one of our primary modern day myths. As a child I watched it faithfully year after year. *The Wizard of Oz* ranks right up there with other ancient and modern journey myths such as *The Iliad* and *The Odyssey, The Epic of Gilgamesh, Where the Wild Things Are,* Star Wars, and Harry Potter to name a few. Like all of these, *The Wizard of Oz* is a hero's journey about returning *home.*

Oz may be a dream world, or at least a portal to the world of dreams. We become cued into this shift in consciousness from life on the farm in Kansas to "not in Kansas anymore" when Dorothy steps over the threshold of her house out into Munchkinland. At that moment, the picture switches suddenly from black and white to living color. With this shift, we too, as viewers, have crossed over some kind of threshold with Dorothy. At the risk of dating myself, I remember when black and white was the only game in town for television, so the sudden living color was even more remarkable. Toward the end of the film, the images blur and shift to black and white once again as Dorothy performs her ritual transition of coming home to Kansas after her journey through Oz. One, two, three; click, click, click.

Is her journey real or imagined? A blow to the head or a mystic dream journey to a place more real than real? Is Dorothy awake or asleep when she travels through the land of Oz? This is left purposefully ambiguous for us to decide, enabling us to be more than merely viewers, also able to participate in the journey.

This journey ultimately brings Dorothy home. Her goal, the holy grail she quests for, is the same one we all have: to get back home. She repeats that intention over and over as she meets her journey companions: the Scarecrow, the Tin Man, the Cowardly Lion, and finally the Wizard himself. They embody the qualities she needs: wisdom, heart, courage, and a wise guide to help her to conquer her fears and navigate this dreamish land that is sometimes frightening but mostly very beautiful, and to reach her heart's desire. The story thus becomes the metaphor to finding your way home by journeying through both your dreams and your fears. This might explain why it has such a deep and enduring resonance. It speaks to the home of our soul.

Oz in Modern-Day Dreams

These Oz companions have become familiar modern-day arche-types (universal larger-than-life symbols) for us, along with the good and wicked witches and the yellow brick road itself. Oz images and characters show up for us in some of our dreams. For example, Karen, a member of one of my dream circles, had a dream where everyone was receiving regular diplomas except for her. Instead, the professor tossed her a pillow covered with seeds. She asked him why everyone else got a diploma, while she only got this pillow.

After working with the dream, Karen recognized that the seeds on her dream pillow represented her own multiple creative gifts, none of which she was really acknowledging in her life and therefore was not bringing to their fullest fruition. Like the Scare-crow, Karen is smart and talented, but wanted that diploma to truly validate it. Pillows, we know, are frequently used when we dream, literally under our heads. So in effect, the pillow turned out to be her special dream diploma containing the seeds of her best, most creative self. Scarecrow was not actually any smarter after receiving his diploma from the Wizard, but with it in his possession he believed in himself. This diploma/pillow empha-sized for Karen that the seeds of her creativity were often found in her dreams.

Like Dorothy, our dreams take us on nighttime journeys to places that are just as real to us while we are asleep as any places we inhabit while awake. They are populated by strange and mag-ical beings, by people known and unknown, by animals real and mythical. They take us on epic adventures and descents to hell and back again. Our dreams take place in this nocturnal world in very real settings, a landscape of the night. Just as Dorothy needed to follow her yellow brick road to find her heart's desire and return home, we too can learn to follow the roadmap that our dreams lay out to guide us home.

Finding Our Way Back Home through Our Dreams

Socrates said, "Know thyself" and that "the unexamined life is not worth living." *Dream tending*, a term coined by Stephen Aizensadt in his book of the same name, allows us to know ourselves more fully; and knowing ourselves is a prerequisite for being at home in our lives. Dreams also allow us to know our dark sides, called the *shadow* in Jungian terms, and integrate them into the wholeness of our being. Shadow is neither good nor bad, but something that is simply a part of us all. It can be that part of ourselves that is unknown, or parts of ourselves that are unacceptable, embarrassing, or fearful to us. Jung tells us that our shadow side is the part of ourselves that is so deeply buried in our unconscious that we experience it as "not me."

The following are examples of shadow showing itself in dreams:

- I dream that I look into the mirror and see an old female version of myself that I barely recognize.

- I dream that a man in a dark cloak is lurking in the shadows, and he feels threatening.

- I dream that a large rhinoceros is blocking my path.

Clarissa Pinkola Estés, author of *Women Who Run With the Wolves: Myths and Stories of the Wild Woman Archetype*, also reminds us that the shadow figure in our dreams can be a message about either our interior or our exterior life. It can be a call to be strong and find ways in our lives to stand up to a predator.

Encountering our shadow in dreams can be a call to arms. Later on we will examine how to work with these shadow parts. Integration of our dark and light sides through dreamwork brings us home to the wholeness of ourselves, just as the wholeness of the yin and yang symbol contains elements of the opposite within each half. We need to acknowledge all the parts of ourselves to be complete. Jung wrote that we don't become enlightened simply by imagining figures of light, but by making the darkness visible.

Dreamworker Jeremy Taylor reminds us that no dreams come simply to tell us something that we already know. Therefore, we can start orienting to our dreams with the assumption that they contain something we don't know yet, even if the dream seems "obvious" at first blush. Some additional knowledge is lurking just below the threshold of our consciousness, waiting to be discovered.

Ally, a colleague of mine, worked on her dream, and subsequently wrote down a list of twenty-two associations to some life issues she thought that the dream might allude to. At the time she did this exercise, she didn't recognize how many of them were relevant for her. She just allowed them to stream out of her. Two years later, she came across that list again in an old file folder. Lo and behold, they were the things she was now working on in therapy. They had been there in her psyche all along; she just had to "find them for herself" as Dorothy did, and wait for the right time for their ripening and fruition. We can't rush the workings of our soul.

What Is "Home"?

Dreams can bring us home, so ask yourself, what is home to you? Two thousand years ago, the Roman philosopher Pliny the Elder said, "Home is where the heart is." Nineteen hundred years later in his poem "The Death of the Hired Man," Robert Frost told us: "Home is the place where, when you have to go there, they have to take you in." Glinda had something to say about this too: "Home is a place we all must find, child. It's not just a place where you eat or sleep. Home is knowing. Knowing your mind, knowing your heart, knowing your courage. If we know ourselves, we're always home, anywhere." Jungian analyst Michael Conforti tells us that a home is "a psychic space where one lives." In different ways, they all tell us that home is within us, or is that which embraces us. I recently booked a vacation getaway through a company called Home-Away. Their marketing is spot on. Even when we go away, we are drawn to the sense of a "home away from home."

Home. It's where we refill and replenish; it is a sense of security, a sense of belonging. We speak about "bringing it all home" when we complete a thought or a project. In many of the games we play as children, the goal is to get *home,* so this concept is ingrained in us early on. In the game "tag," you are safe when you get to home base. Same for capture the flag. Same for Parcheesi. In backgammon you have to get all your pieces to your *home quarter* before you can begin taking them off the board for a win. Same for baseball. We round the bases towards home, and hitting a home run is as good as it gets!

The turtle and the snail are always at home wherever they are—they literally carry their homes on their backs. We too can benefit from the skill of being able to access the feeling of being home at a moment's notice, as they do. However, so many of us still seek that place of refuge, of belonging, that can seem so elusive. Perhaps most importantly, we need to feel at home inside ourselves. Knowing yourself well enough—your own heart, your own mind, and your own courage, to say that you are at home inside your own skin is a deep teaching of many spiritual disciplines. Working with our dreams brings us into contact with our deepest and fullest selves, perhaps the closest to the core of our being, our true home base, that we can get this side of the grave.

Our dreams and even our nightmares contain seeds that make us able to come into relationship with our own essence, our highest and wisest self. Dreams can provide us with practical answers, show us a path for healing, connect us with the Divine, provide creative juice, and even see around the corners of time to events that have not yet happened. If we learn to follow the yellow brick road of the clues strewn amidst the landscapes and characters in our dreams, we find our deepest home. Like a compass that will point the way to true north, the compass of our dreams will always point us to our truest home.

Mindful Dreaming and Dreams as Orientation

Mindfulness. It's become a buzzword. Masters and teachers of this practice such as the Dalai Lama and Jon Kabat-Zinn speak of mindfulness as the ability to be fully present in this moment of here and now. As we dive more deeply into this concept, we can learn to be mindful before, during, and after dreaming. Mindful, attentive dreamwork enriches the information we receive from our dreams. Retelling our dreams in the present tense, as if they are happening just now, is one way of being mindful. And mindfulness in our waking life closes this circuit and enhances our sense of being at home in ourselves.

To be home in yourself is to be present, and to be present is to be aware, noticing what is around you in this moment, not distracted or pulled into our stories of what was (your past) or what might be (your future). Mindfulness is also the ability to be in the center of one's own life. "Self-energy," a state of calm self-awareness, is the term used in the therapeutic modality of IFS (Internal Family Systems). IFS developer Richard Schwartz identifies the poetic "Cs" of consciousness, curiosity, compassion, centeredness, clarity, and connection that can help to bring us home to ourselves.

We have all had the experience of getting lost or of losing our sense of direction at least metaphorically, if not literally. To find ourselves again, to find our way home, we first need to be able to reorient ourselves. To do so, we need to either spot a familiar landmark or receive directions. Then we need to get back on track or find a new direction. In many sports and in politics this is called "course correction." In archery and boating it's called "sighting." We need to sight, or orient ourselves toward where we want our canoe or our arrow to go, and then make any necessary corrections in our trajectory if we've gone off course. Dreams are our internal navigational system that check our course in life and offer us options for recalibration.

If we are "off course" in our lives, our dreaming self will offer us course correction to get back on track. If we pay attention to our dream messages, explore the layers of meaning embedded even in the seemingly simplest dreams, and then take some waking action based on our new understanding, we recalibrate and orient toward our true direction. Here is an example of how a dream helped me with course correction, starting first with a related "waking course correction" to clarify the concept.

I love to swim, but for years I always swam crooked—no matter how I tried to orient myself to the pool lane, or to some landmark on the shore, I always ended up swimming at an angle and couldn't figure out why. One day while swimming at Walden Pond I mentioned this to my friend Anne, who was a swim instructor. It was a hot summer day, and we were lazily swimming across the lake together. We turned face to face doing sidestroke to talk, and she said, "Maybe one arm is stronger than the other, and could be pulling you off course. If that's the problem, you just have to compensate for it."

That advice immediately rang true. I replied, "I am a very strong lefty; my right hand is practically incapable of even opening a bottle cap. Thanks so much. I'll start paying attention to that." As I did so, I noticed that I did always veer to the left when swimming. But until Anne pointed it out to me, I hadn't noticed it. Now I could begin to correct my course. I began to give a few extra strong pulls with my right arm every few strokes to correct for the imbalance. Recently I noticed that I rarely have to do that anymore: with years of practice, my stroke has evened out. More often than not I am swimming pretty straight. It seems I have finally internalized this learning and now am unconsciously making the needed correction. We all have times when we aren't able to figure out what is needed in our life, or what our dream is telling us. I needed that swim instructor to evaluate my stroke to tell me why I was veering off course; I hadn't been able to figure it out by myself. But that was her area of expertise, so she diagnosed the problem rather quickly. After I knew what the problem was, I was able to adapt and figure out a solution.

Here is how this can work for dream-guided course correction. Staying with the theme of swimming, several years ago I developed arthritis in my neck (true, aging is not for sissies). I was saddened to think that I may have to give up swimming altogether, as the turning-the-head-to-breathe part of the crawl stroke quickly became painful. To seek a solution to this dilemma, I asked for a dream to help me. The dream I got a few days later was simple—it told me, *"Swim like a fish."*

That was it, the whole dream. I had an image of a fish, and those words. I knew it was connected to what I had asked, since it was fairly obvious that it was about swimming, but I didn't know at first what it was trying to tell me. What about fish, or swimming like them, could help with arthritis in my neck? Unless I could magically grow a set of gills that dream would be of little help.

Weeks went by and I still wasn't able to decipher this clue. Then I remembered that a year earlier I had been snorkeling off the coast of Mexico while on vacation. I had been mesmerized by the beautiful underwater world of fish and coral for over an hour and my neck hadn't bothered me. "Aha, that's it!" I exclaimed as the realization struck home. I had been wearing my snorkel and mask, and therefore didn't need to turn my head to breathe. This was my answer. I don't need to grow gills to swim like a fish, just to keep my head on straight. Fairly straightforward, but I had to figure it out in my own time.

I now bring my snorkel and mask with me wherever I swim— to the pool at my gym, to the lake at dance camp, to the ocean beaches on the north shore of Boston. I can swim without suffering, a practical solution gifted to me by my dream. Aging will not slow me down that fast. Our dreams can show us how to adapt to the changing circumstances of our lives.

Dreams and Symbols

To use an analogy, symbol is to dream as word is to language. We understand the meaning of a language through the words we use, and we often understand the meanings of our dreams through the symbols they use. In addition, our dream symbols can contain multiple meanings, just as a single word can have many meanings ranging from the literal to metaphorical or analogous. The word *run*, for example, can mean to move ones legs very quickly, or a flaw that appears, often quickly, in a stocking. A dream might also show a run in a stocking as a symbol meaning to "run away from" a situation, possibly something embarrassing, much as a run in a stocking could be embarrassing if you have an important presentation to make and want to look your best.

Spring is the season following winter; it can also describe a coiled metal wire, a surprise, or the action of hopping or jumping. The meaning of the symbols depends both on the context in the dream and the associations of the dreamer. So if you dreamed of a coiled wire, it could imply any of these, or other more personal meanings.

We share universal human experiences and cultural commonalities. Therefore, some symbols have a fairly universal resonance that could hold true for your own dreams. Think about your personal associations to a dream image, as well as considering universal meanings and how it could be used as symbol, metaphor, analogy, or a play on words.

For example, after discussing water and fish in the previous example, we can bring water back as a symbol that often has universal resonance. Water in the lexicon of dream symbols is frequently a metaphor for the unconscious mind. It is then symbolic of our inner depths and the parts of ourselves that we don't yet know consciously. A dream can contain water in its literal sense, such as an ocean or lake, but we can also understand it figuratively as representing our inner depths, anything under the surface. Your own emotional resonance will also affect the meaning of the symbol for you. If you are a non-swimmer, or an anxious one, water may imply feeling "out of your depth." As Freud tells us, sometimes "a cigar is just a cigar" in a dream, but sometimes it means something else entirely, such as a phallic symbol, a smoke-screen, or a foul odor.

The only authentic meaning of a dream is that which resonates as true for the dreamer. This bears repeating: The true meaning of any dream symbol is that which resonates as true to the dreamer. We will give deeper attention to symbolism later, but for now let's bookmark the topic by stating that seeking out the viewpoints of friends and dream dictionaries can be helpful, but always take them with a healthy grain of salt. Without your own personal "aha," that shiver or tingle of truth at the bone, it's probably not true for you. This tingle or aha may be a function of memory. At some level we recognize that we already knew this, like a déjà vu of the night, and that we are remembering something that was previously buried, as it rises to consciousness in our dream.

Connecting Dream and Myth

Jungian analysts Marie-Louise von Franz and Clarissa Pinkola Estés expand our look at the universality of dream symbols to include the larger world stories of myth and sacred literature. They encourage us to become familiar with myth and story from many cultures to expand our repertoire of universal symbolism. Archetypes, those deep universal motifs propelling us toward inner balance, can be reflected in our dreams.

In her work entitled "On Dreams and Dying," von Franz tells us, "The unconscious thinks in mythological terms. That's why it is valuable to have a large mythological context of material to draw from. If we can learn to think in symbolic terms ... then it's easier to understand the dream message. The dream function doesn't seem to differ between outer world and inner, archetypal and personal." Sacred literature, mythos, and fairy tales from around the world and across time speak of the numinous (the sacred) appearing through dreams and visions, confirming von Franz's thesis.

Estés tells us that stories are medicine, and we know that dreams are stories. In her book *Women Who Run with the Wolves*, Estés makes explicit the connections between myth and dream, all of which resonate in our deep life of the spirit: "Fairy tales, folktales, legends, and mythos … contain instruction for our lives … [and our] dreams are portals, entrances, preparations, and practices for the next step in … consciousness." Dreams can be windows into higher and deeper levels of consciousness. Eden Phillpotts, in his book *A Shadow Passes*, states, "The universe is full of magic things, patiently waiting for our sense to grow sharper."

Dreaming Across Cultures

Spiritual traditions the world over have looked at dreams as portals into a spiritual or sacred realm. Many Native American traditions emphasize the importance of both spontaneous dreams and those dreams or visions that come through on a vision quest, one of the primary transition rites to adulthood. The young man or woman goes off alone for a period of time with the hopes of having a dream or vision to find their true name and a direction that will guide them for the rest of their life. The capacity to dream, and to dream strong with messages for the tribe, is a central spiritual value in many Native traditions.

Australian Aboriginal creation mythology tells us that the world was dreamed into being. This "dreaming the world into existence" was called dreamtime. It came about as the Spirit Beings placed what they called song lines; invisible lines of power and place, down onto the earth. Centuries later, Jean Houston, human potential scholar and author, wrote about the dreamtime in her book *A Mythic Life*. She interprets dreamtime as "the depth world flowing through this one. It is always and never; a time that never was and is always happening."

The original storytellers taught their children that the world was sung and dreamed into being. Sitting at night out under the stars, they tell that in the beginning the spirits of the dream moved out over the land, singing the earth into being. These dream spirits took the shape of the native animals, who then gave their names and corresponding gifts to the clans that carry their spirit. This is part of the meaning of "totem animal"—the animal with power of flight or far-sightedness or swiftness graces us with their gifts.

The spirit songs put down paths of power on the earth, called ley lines. Each invisible ley line is connected with its own totem animal. The journeys of each clan follow the line of their own totem animal. Their history is preserved and passed down through the stories, art, songs, and dances that reflect this dreamtime. This oral tradition of song lines is an ancient memory code or mnemonic device used by indigenous cultures around the world.

Eastern and Western cultures both speak of night dreams and day visions in many of their sacred books. In Western religious writings, we learn of the importance of dreams to the ancient Egyptians from the biblical story of Joseph. He is brought forth from imprisonment to interpret the pharaoh's dreams, thus securing himself a place as the pharaoh's chief advisor. Joseph also saved the ancient world from widespread famine through his correct interpretation of the dream of the seven fat and the seven lean cows. His subsequent dream-based action step of stockpiling grain in silos to use during the seven lean years was directly based on his understanding of the dream symbols.

The Judeo-Christian Bible has multiple references to both waking visions and night dreams. In the original Hebrew the same word is often used for both: *chalom* (rhymes with *shalom*). It can mean either dream or vision, depending on its context. Here are a few examples where this multipurpose word *chalom* is used. After Joseph, perhaps the most well-known biblical dreamer is Jacob. He dreamed (called in the Hebrew, chalom), when he fell asleep with his head on a stone of the stairway to heaven, a ladder between heaven and earth with angels traveling up and down it. When Elijah hears the "still small Voice" of God speaking to him, it is at the selfsame spot where Moses earlier had the vision of the burning bush. The word *chalom* is used again. Elijah was wide awake when he heard the voice of God. In this instance, *chalom* is translated as "vision," thereby letting us know that he was fully awake hearing the voice.

Ezekiel is the third book of the section Prophets in the Tanach, the Old Testament. In chapter 1 of this book Ezekiel dreams of a mystical chariot with four different animals as its four wheels, hinting at an image of God. This vision is later commemorated in the African American spiritual song, "Ezekiel Saw the Wheel": "Ezekiel saw a wheel a'turning, way in the middle of the air..." This vision serves as one of the bases for the most mystical branch of Kabbalah. Islam also has a strong tradition of attention to dreaming, and those writing about the life of Muhammad speak of his dream revelations and prophecies. We see that dreams and visions are closely related; both contain the numinous, and both present messages for our lives.

Turning to the east, Vishnu, one of the major gods of the Hindu pantheon, dreams that a wonderful lotus grows out of his navel and the universe arises from it. According to Kelley Bulkeley in his book *Dreaming in the World's Religions*, "The meaning of this is to say that ... we create whole worlds out of dream matter." In Buddhism, a core creation story is the conception dream of Queen Maya, who dreams of being impregnated by a sacred white elephant.

The Function and Purpose of Dreams

Dreams can do their work to help us integrate and metabolize the events our lives, even if we don't understand exactly how they do so. The following are some typical dream functions:

Memory Consolidation: Dreaming helps us integrate the learning that we have done during the day. Dreams assist us with information storage and memory processing. Dreams also provide a forum in which we can plan or rehearse new actions or ideas. This can activate and grow new neural networks in our brains, and like good gardeners, our dreams can prune away those that we no longer need. In other words, we can dream to remember, and we can dream to forget. "Let me sleep on it" is a valid response to problem-solving and decision-making.

Compensation: Classically, this refers to a psychic adjustment that our unconscious makes for us while we are asleep. It can help us integrate events of the day, aiding us in adapting to the changing circumstances in our life. Dream compensation attempts to sensitize us to aspects of ourselves that we are not aware of, targeting the blind spots we all have and then making adjustments needed for balance. Our dreams can provide us with a snapshot of the current state of our being: our mental, emotional, and even physical self. As the dreams help us let off steam in our sleep, they thus return our system to a more balanced state of internal homeostasis. This is one of the functions of dreams that serves to bring us home.

For example, my client Deborah has trouble expressing anger in her waking life; she describes herself as "conflict avoidant." In her compensatory dream, she got very angry at someone, and in the dream screamed at him that she hated conflict. Because she avoids conflict to a fault in waking life, this dream points out the irony of yelling about hating conflict.

Precognitive: This refers to potential awareness of future events, a type of future consciousness that lets us dream something before it happens. Like a weather report, it is not always exact, but can serve to let us see around the corners of time a bit, to have a heads-up and thus be able to better prepare. Some strong dreamers are gifted with not only the ability to see future events for themselves, but to get insights for loved ones through their dreams.

Telepathic: Related to precognitive dreams, this type allows us to connect with the minds of others. Each year the International Dream Conference of the International Association for the Study of Dreams (IASD) holds a dream telepathy contest, where a volunteer concentrates strongly on an image in a picture before going to sleep and the rest of the conference attendees are invited to try to dream of the image the volunteer is concentrating on. It constantly amazes me how close some dreamers get to the target image. This kind of mind-meld can happen spontaneously as well.

Prodromal: Dreams can be sources of healing, and a type of dream known as *prodromal dream* has been known to provide health reports even before a problem shows up on medical testing. For example, Stan had recurring dreams about having plumbing problems in his house or his office over and over, with increasing urgency. In the first dreams there were drips, and in the next ones he couldn't turn off the faucets, and finally the drains clogged up. Because of our awareness that dreams have a potential layer of reference to our physical bodies, the dream group urged him to check out these "plumbing issues" with his doctor. Testing showed early prostate cancer, which was still in the very treatable stage, thanks to early detection by his dreams.

Reductive: Some schools of dreamwork reduce everything in a dream to one orientation or interpretation. For followers of Freud, it may be sexual; for Adler it may be power; for Jung it may be spiritual. My own orientation is not to approach the dream from a single framework, but to consider many options and meanings. I do want to consider these three big ideas, but I prefer not to be limited by just one theory.

Reactive: These dreams occur in reaction to something that has happened in our lives. The stimulus for these dreams is a life event that is registering neurologically. It can be quite literally a replay of events that occurred as our system digests and integrates them. If they are pleasant events, we enjoy the instant replay. If the dreams are recurring nightmares, then we have not yet metabolized the unpleasant or traumatic life event sufficiently to put it to rest (so to speak). Persistent negative reactive dreams may need outside consultation to resolve.

Creative Resource: We get inspiration through our dreams for art, music, writing, and dance. They connect us with our muses and tell us stories. Some of the greatest artists of all time attribute their inspirations directly to their dreams. Paul McCartney, Amadeus Mozart, and Marc Chagall come immediately to mind. We will devote a whole chapter to this later.

Portals: Many people believe that our dreams can be portals through which we travel to other worlds and connect with our departed loved ones, with the Divine, and with other spiritual beings, guides, and realms. At the very least, our dreams are portals into other states of being or ways of knowing.

Understanding and working with the many layers and functions of our dreams allows us to engage in multitasking at its best—we get to sleep and solve problems or have adventures simultaneously. Let us now dive into your dreams and continue this journey together to the land of "infinite possibilities." We'll focus next on how to remember our dreams, a prerequisite to working on them.

EXERCISE

Think or journal about the meaning of home for you. Spend some time reflecting on where you have lived and where you have felt "at home" in the most personal meaningful sense. Some of us feel most at home inside a house or building, others outside in nature in a special hidden spot, still others in a place of worship. Notice whether you carry your sense of home inside or outside of yourself. That is, does something in your world remind you of, or make you feel at home, or is it some inner state of emotion or sensation for you? Some people feel at home when they recognize that they are calm and relaxed, or when they have a peaceful or loving feeling in their heart or their belly. Pay attention to your kinesthetic as well as emotional and cognitive indicators.

Notice if you dream about houses. What makes a place feel like home to you? For some, it is the furnishings or the pictures on the wall or mantle. For others it is the people who are there. For others, it may be a sense of connection with something sacred or larger than yourself. It might be favorite foods, or certain smells. This might be an occasion to practice mindful awareness of home base, as preparation for honing in on it in your dreams.

Reflect also on the theme of orientation—that concept of sighting or course correction. How does that work in your own waking and dreaming life? How do you notice if you are "off course" somewhere? Write some about that too. If you have received advice or suggestions about how to get back on track from professionals, friends, or your own dreams or journaling, what do you typically do when you get inner or outer suggestions? Finally, as you begin to catch more dreams, see whether these themes resonate for you at this particular time in your life.

Two

THE ART OF STRONG DREAMING: DREAM RECALL

"The value of regular dream-recall for writers
is that it makes us aware of the continuous
flow of stories and images moving through
us all the time, like an underground stream."
Jenny Alexander

We need our dreams. Without them, we lose a crucial part of our innate ability to process and metabolize the experiences in our lives. As we learned in the last chapter, dreams help us with memory consolidation. Our dreams contain wisdom to help in making crucial decisions, and also for improving our recall and memory of events learned during the day. This is a part of why a good night's sleep before a big test is so helpful. In addition to being well rested, our dreaming brains actually retain more firmly the information we studied the day before. Several Harvard University dream and memory researchers confirm this thesis in their studies.

Dreams also help us work through difficult emotions and life events. They allow us to reprocess the material, get more distance from it, and hopefully become desensitized to it so we have less reactivity. When nightmares persist, we may need additional help, as we will explore in chapter 11. As a therapist, I always encourage my clients to start a dream journal and catch their dreams. This adds an immeasurable amount of richness to their work in therapy.

Sleep and brain studies confirm that we do dream every night. So when we say, "I don't dream," what we really mean is, "I don't remember my dream." Neurological PET scans of the brain in sleep labs have clearly shown that we all have four to seven sleep cycles, called REM cycles, nightly (REM stands for rapid eye movement, the quick movements our eyelids make when we are in the dreaming part of this cycle). This is predicated on an average of seven to eight hours of sleep per night. If you are one of the lucky ones who can still function well on less sleep, then you probably have fewer cycles. (My husband, for example, rarely sleeps more than six hours, and can function quite well on five. I, on the other hand, need that full eight hours to be at my best, and am happy when I can occasionally snatch a ninth). We generally only remember the dreams that occur in the cycle right before we wake up.

"Strong Dreaming"

There are several ways to understand the concept of "strong dreaming." Some strong dreamers are those who frequently catch multiple dreams per night. Mia, a member of my dream circle, is such a dreamer. She ultimately devised a shorthand system of notation to jot down keywords from the four to six dreams she remembered each night and then used her notes to write them out more fully in the morning.

Another type of strong dreaming is the out-of-body experience, in which the dreamer witnesses what is happening from above. This experience has been reported both in nocturnal dreams and in conscious and unconscious near-death experiences. It may not register on our medical equipment, but has been frequently reported anecdotally.

An additional variation on strong dreaming is called lucid dreaming. These dreamers have the ability to recognize that they are having a dream while in the middle of actually dreaming it, both spontaneously or through practice. They have the sensation of being awake while they are asleep, and experience an awareness that they are dreaming while in the middle of their dream; sort of a "meta" layer of the dream. This skill can be learned with practice and can empower the dreamer, especially with nightmares.

Other strong dreamers have the ability to pick up on cues from their waking surroundings while asleep. These cues somehow penetrate their dreams and provide them with information. We see these concepts in fantasy fiction too. Many of our fantasy writers cross the threshold between waking and dreaming in order to generate their insights and visions. They either engage in lucid dreaming themselves as source material for their work, or have their characters do so. J. K. Rowling has Harry Potter, in *Harry Potter and the Order of the Phoenix*, do this. He lucidly dreams that the snake avatar of "He-Who-Must-Not-Be-Named" is attacking his friend Ron Weasley's father, just as the attack is actually happening. He thus is able to alert members of the Order to get to Mr. Weasley quickly enough to save his life. Harry thus combines a level of lucid dreaming with the ability to tune in to the environment while dreaming.

Our cave men and women ancestors and the tribespeople of indigenous cultures counted on the strong dreamers of their clan to use their dream radar and extend their consciousness beyond the cave to be on the alert for potential danger. Our dreams link us back to our ancestors through this shared collective knowledge. In dreamtime, we too have the ability to extend our consciousness to the waking world, alerting us as it alerted our ancestors to the saber-toothed tiger or the approaching storm that they needed to make some preparations for.

It has been documented frequently that animals are the ones first seen running for high ground to avoid the incoming waters of the tsunami or the flames of the creeping forest fire long before humans have picked up the danger. This skill is still latent within us, but oft disbelieved or neglected. It perhaps shows up most often these days with our children. Many parents report that they tap into this sixth sense when they wake suddenly at night, somehow alerted in sleep to the slightest sound or intimation that their child may need them.

While I was camping in the White Mountains with some friends for a weekend I had this dream: I suddenly woke in the night, hearing and seeing the ambulance lights flashing from my dream. My immediate waking thought was "I hope my husband and daughter are alright."

I had no way to check though until the next day when we got back into cell phone range. When I was able to reach home, my daughter told me that my husband had a bike accident and an ambulance came to take him to the hospital (luckily not life-threatening). My dream radar showed me those ambulance lights right after the event occurred.

Precognitive dreaming is another form of strong dreaming. There are times when we dream of events before they occur, probably more often than we realize. They are not always big life-shattering events, but can also be our small daily occurrences. Recently I dreamt that a large tree came down by the roots near my house, but that luckily the houses weren't damaged. Two days later we had a major nor'easter storm, and that exact tree from my dream was uprooted one block away. (And, as predicted by my dream, the houses weren't damaged.) We may not remember these precognitive dreams, however, if we do not write them down.

Sometimes strong dreaming can be delightful, but it can also be exhausting, uncanny, or frightening. Knowing that it is a part of our inherited legacy can help us appreciate it, respect it, and learn to use it well.

Why Can't I Remember My Dreams?

The state of sleep in many ways is the ultimate test of not being in control. Anxiety can prevent us from relaxing into slumber. We need to have a certain amount of trust to voluntarily allow ourselves to be so out of control that we truly are not even conscious of where we are (aka the state of being asleep), and excess anxiety can certainly interfere with trust. Spiritual author and counselor Byron Katie tells us that we need three kinds of trust to make our way well in the world: trust in ourselves, trust in others, and trust in the universe. When one or more of those is missing, we need to heal the parts of ourselves that have lost this birthright. So if the ability to fall asleep is in part an issue of trust for us, the assistance of calming, soothing, and protecting rituals before bedtime may help us relax into the arms of sleep so that we can remember our dreams. Whatever helps you feel safe at night can be used:

a bedtime prayer, surrounding yourself with light, checking to be sure you have locked the doors, a warm bath, or a cup of tea.

There are many things that may interfere with our ability to remember our dreams. Drugs of all kinds may be the first culprits—certain prescription medications, recreational drugs, and definitely sleep aids or sedatives could all have an effect. Our insomniac culture has come to rely more and more on pharmaceutical sleeping aids that allow us to sleep at the expense of restorative dreaming. There was a period of time in my life when I suffered from insomnia. Although this pharmacopeia of choices allowed me to get some rest, I felt cut off from my dreaming life. I noticed during this time that I was only able to remember one or two dreams a month at the most. Prior to that I could usually catch several dreams each week in my journal. Caffeine and alcohol can both interfere with our sleep and our dreams. Most of us know that caffeine too close to bedtime can interfere with sleep, but that nightcap can also dull our dreaming brain even though that may seem counterintuitive.

Ambient light in our rooms can also impede our sleep. Lights from our ubiquitous screens, the LED light from our alarm clock, or any kind of lit up plug-in can interfere. We are not yet sure how computers may affect our dreams or our sleep, or our brains for that matter, so it is prudent to have them closed and away from our heads. Keeping our screens off and our lights covered can help. We can also invest in a small eyeshade to preserve the darkness.

Does Depression Affect Our Dreams?

We actually need our deep dreaming sleep for our physical and our emotional health. We are currently experiencing an "epidemic of sleep and dream deprivation" in our modern culture.

Since the 1960s, research has shown that loss of REM/dream sleep results in health concerns including "depression, weight gain, hallucinations ... erosion of reason, memory ... immune system functions ... and a loss of spirituality," according to Dr. Matthew Walker in his book *Why We Sleep*. Having good solid sleep that gets us to REM/dream stage helps the brain process traumatic events. We've heard of the saying "time heals all wounds." Since dreams help us process what has happened in our lives over time, we can also say that dreaming helps us heal our wounds. Walker also notes that, "Dreaming mollifies painful memories and creates a virtual reality space in which the brain melds past and present knowledge to inspire creativity."

Dreams are a mirror of our emotional state, and the emotional resonance of the dream is what stays with us. The affect present in a dream can make the difference between the same dream being alternately experienced as entertaining, scary, sad, or confusing. Depression and other mood disorders affect our cognitions and our emotions, and can interfere with our dreams. In fact, lack of dream recall is one of the typical features of depression. In addition to persisting negative thoughts, feelings, and physical signs of depression, such as a loss of appetite, loss of interest in participating in life, and loss of energy, the lack of REM sleep can be both a symptom and cause of depression.

Rosalind Cartwright's research on the brain shows that REM sleep may actually be disrupted in people suffering from depression; it begins too early in our sleep cycle and lasts too long. Dreams contain a mood-regulating function. When this regulatory metabolic function is not being properly accessed, we are unable to utilize our nocturnal processing to modulate our emotions or repair our psyche. When someone who reports being depressed is able to gain or regain access to their dreams, they often simultaneously report a lifting of the depression. This does not happen overnight; sometimes our system needs weeks or months to reorganize.

My client Lisa had suffered a number of losses in her life. Her mother died when she was five and she lost her father when she was twenty-two. She came to therapy at twenty-eight when she had finished graduate school and had recently broken up with her boyfriend. Lisa had no idea what to do next, or if she even wanted a career in the field she had studied. She had grown up in a buttoned-up stoic family system. When each of her parents died, she was told, "Just get over it; no use crying about it." Needless to say, she was not encouraged or supported by her family in her grieving. By the time she started therapy at twenty-eight, the unprocessed grief had become internalized to a chronic low-level depression.

Among other things, I asked Lisa to keep a dream journal to help her climb out of this depression. When she told me that she "never" dreamed, I explained to her the science of dreaming, and that while she didn't remember her dreams yet, they were in there. The addition of the word "yet" to accessing a resource for practically any dilemma or stuck place opens up a whole world of possibilities. She was willing to try, so I suggested that if she ever awoke with the sense that she might have had a dream, even if she couldn't remember anything about it, to simply write the date down in her dream journal, and the words "had a dream" next to it.

After a few weeks of faithfully keeping her journal by her bed, she came in excited to report that she was conscious of having had a dream that week, even though she recalled nothing of the content "yet." The very fact that she was excited about this was already a good sign, signifying a small break in her flat grey wall of depression. And sure enough, a few weeks later, she recalled the contents of her first dream in years.

This didn't just happen "overnight" though. Lisa focused her desire to remember her dreams for several weeks before she was able to remember them. She developed the practice of attending to her dreaming self. As we continued to work with and process her dreams, she had more and more vitality, and reported her depression lifting.

Dream Enhancement

There are herbs, medicinal plants, and hallucinogens that can have been used over the ages to enhance dreaming. Native cultures often used herbs such as ayahuasca in ritual fashion on vision quests as a means of opening a portal to the spirit world. Carlos Castaneda famously wrote of the peyote-inspired dreams of his character don Juan. The herb mugwort is frequently mentioned as a dream enhancer today.

In my search for a mild non-prescription sleep aid, I once found a valerian-poppy tincture in the aisles of a natural food store. "This is all natural, it should be fine," I thought. I slept well, and as a bonus, had especially vivid dreams. When I reported this discovery to my dream circle, they reminded me what poppies were. "Oh yeah, poppies"—the seed plant of some powerful narcotics. No wonder I had eye-popping dreams that night. That field of poppies had a strongly soporific effect on Dorothy, Toto, and the Lion when the Wicked Witch of the West wanted to prevent their entry to Oz. (They were the only flesh and blood members of her posse, so the Scarecrow and the Tin Man weren't affected.) They conked out halfway through the poppy field with the towers of the Emerald City right in sight. Glinda saved the day once again by making it snow on the sleeping mammals to awaken them from their poppy-induced slumber.

In traditional cultures the most respected men and women were often the strongest dreamers. Receiving a powerful dream was often part of the requirement to become a priest or shaman, and tribal leaders frequently consulted their strongest dreamers for advice and direction. Leaders and shamans were asked to dream not only for themselves, but for the good of the tribe as well. Their ability to dream strong was part of what elevated their status.

Today we may suffer a lack of connection with our dreams as a result of drinking or medicating them away, but also because of devaluing them and not attending to them. This has both personal and societal implications. This inattention to our dreams reflects how out of touch our world often seems to be with the deep spiritual wisdom that the best of our elders and traditions can offer us. We would be well served to re-establish our connections and respect for non-linear ways of learning and knowing, such as dreaming.

How to Remember Your Dreams

There are many techniques and methods that can enhance dream recall. First and foremost, you have to *want* to remember them and really put value on them. It may seem obvious, but if you think about it, we tend to remember things better when they are important to us and we value them. Before dozing off, tell yourself that you want to remember your dreams, and make the commitment to yourself that you will pay attention to the messages they are sending you. You can write this commitment in your dream journal, or speak it out loud or silently. Marcia, one of my dream circle members, once hypothesized that she was not remembering or recording her dreams lately because her life was so full of transition and turmoil at the moment that she just didn't want to remember them right now. A mental block like this can sometimes be the case.

Next, visualize yourself remembering your dreams. Athletes are often coached to imagine a play-by-play successful touchdown or field goal to achieve prowess in their sport. In that way, our body/mind puts the desired process in motion as a form of rehearsal. This technique of preemptive visualization works for dream recall as well. The visualization might be something like:

> "I see myself waking up in the morning before my alarm clock rings with a clear dream in my mind. I remember to hold very still to 'set' it, and then I carefully turn over onto my left side where my dream journal is and reach for it slowly. I pick up my pen and write my dream down. I am able to remember all the details."

This is also part of dream incubation, which we will investigate in more detail in the next chapter. Once you have primed the pump and have started remembering, you can also use this technique to ask for help and guidance on specific issues or dilemmas.

Invest in a journal and keep it right next to your bed, along with a pen or sharpened pencil. Choose a style of journal that gives you some pleasure so you will be more inclined to reach for it. As far as writing implements go, both online and at most office supply stores you can even get special pens that light up in the dark. The most critical aspect of your writing implement is that your pens have ink or that your pencils be sharpened. Your unconscious will know that you aren't really serious about remembering if you neglect to make sure your tools are in working order! As you record your dreams, date each entry. That way you begin to have a chronological record of dreams and themes that reoccur, and can check them against what was going on in your life that day or week to get some immediate connections and insights when you go back to work on them.

Dreams are like helium balloons—they need to be tied down to stay with us or they float away. Anchor them by writing or recording them right away. The vast majority of us forget our dreams shortly after waking. Although there are occasional dreams that stay with us long after we have dreamt them, most dreams have the substance of shadowy mist or wisps of smoke. They need to be solidified in writing or recorded orally to gain enough traction to remain in the waking world. The more solid we can make them, the more we can grasp and work with what they have come to teach us. If you chose to record your dreams in an online journal, the same principle holds: be sure that your device is charged and near your bed.

We also must recognize that dreams do not come only in words. If you wake with a feeling state that is not explained by your immediate environment, that may be what you are recalling from your dream. Wake inexplicably happy? That is your dream. Wake feeling anxious for no apparent reason? That too is your dream. Record these things as well. The feeling states in your dreams are a primary signpost to the idiosyncratic meaning of your dream to you. Wake with an image or a picture in your mind's eye? You may be more of a visual person than a narrative one. That is your dream too. Record this either in words or in a sketch/drawing.

When you awaken, try to move as little as possible while you reach for your recording materials, to prevent disturbing the fragile fabric of your dream state. Sit up slowly, or even write while still lying down. If you had a dream and it slipped away, try putting your body back into the same position it was in when you woke—your body has "positional memory" and you can often recapture the dream if you return to the same position. For example, if you were sleeping on your left side with your knees curled up and your hands tucked under your chin, recreate that exact position to try to recall the dream. Stay in that position for a few moments—it sometimes takes your body a little time to recover its memory of what it was doing when last in that position. It constantly amazes me how well this technique works. The word *remember* can be broken down into "re" and "member." A member is a body part, often a limb, so we are literally putting our bodies back together again when we re-member with it.

Try to write down your dream in the same order in which you dreamed it—what happened first, next, and last in a dream sequence makes a difference when you are working with it later. Sometimes though, the only hook that we have back into the dream is to start at the ending. If you are afraid that you will forget it if you don't write down the end first, go ahead and do so, but then rewrite it in order, or at least make some arrows and notations so you know the chronological order in which you actually dreamed the scenes. Some of my own dream entries are replete with arrows and notations as I scurry to capture it before it is lost.

If you find yourself starting to analyze your dream as you are writing or recording it, I suggest that you wait until you have finished writing it down. Otherwise it can get confusing to sort out later on what was actually your dream and what were your thoughts about your dream. If you have some immediate associations at this stage that you don't want to lose, create a separate section called "notes" or "thoughts" and write them there. Your waking associations and ideas can contaminate the unadulterated dream material, and you don't want to lose the pure access to your unconscious process by mixing it with conscious thought at this juncture.

The Practice of Dream Recall

Dream recall is like any other routine—it gets better with time and practice. Buddhist teacher and scholar Thich Nhat Hanh has written and spoken of mindfulness practices throughout the world. He said that people expect him to be really good at it since he teaches worldwide, but that his own mindfulness practice still takes a lot of work. At a workshop I attended in Boston, he said that we all spend so much time every day being sad, angry, or unconscious that we give these states of being a lot of practice. He encouraged us not to spend so much time practicing suffering, but rather to practice joy and equanimity. Similarly, the more we practice dream recall the more skilled we will become at it.

It is perfectly normal to have periods of time when you remember many dreams, and then dry periods when you can't capture any. It could be that your daily life is so full at the moment that there is no room in your psyche for more information to come through. Or you may already be working deeply in your waking life (in therapy, in journaling, or in deep conversation, for example), so that your dream muse feels that your inner life is being covered for now.

Learning to recognize the many forms a dream may take can also help our practice. Not all dreams take the form of narratives with a clear storyline. Some do, to be sure, but some are one-liners. One line remembered from sleep is a dream. (If you recall, my whole dream in chapter 1 was simply "Swim like a fish"). One phrase counts. So does a single word. Don't dismiss these dream fragments—often they contain the essence of the message your dreaming mind is sending you in a crisp *Reader's Digest* format. A single word or phrase can contain worlds. In addition, we can have dreams in the liminal in-between zones of waking and sleeping called the hypnopompic and the hypnogogic zones. Here in this space where we are not quite awake or not quite asleep—these are dreams too. Write down these drowsy thoughts as well; they are formulated in the same parts of our brain that our fully nocturnal dreams come from.

Appendix I at the end of this book will also provide you with a summary and additional means to enhance dream recall.

Harnessing Dream Overload

Although most of us struggle more with not being able to remember our dreams, some people are conversely overwhelmed by the amount or length of them. They become exhausted by the sheer volume and need a break. If you are one of those copious dreamers, you can endeavor to contain your dreams prior to going to sleep. You might use your dream journal to write down your goal of allowing through only the dreams of highest priority and filtering out anything else. It might be, "I will remember only the dream that is in my highest good and best interest," or "My strong mind and dream muse will screen out any dream that threatens to overwhelm my system or that I am not ready to cope with."

Use the language that works best for you. This method can work to contain some nightmares too, until you have the resources to work with them. Chapter 11 will provide more guidance on healing nightmares.

A Native American tradition is to hang a woven circular creation called a dreamcatcher near your bed. The story that accompanies these ritual objects is that the dreamcatcher snares any upsetting dreams or nightmares in its threads. The narrow hole that is in the center of authentic dreamcatchers serves to allow only positive dreams to slip through and then down the hanging threads or feathers to the sleeper underneath. You can also "infuse" your dreamcatcher to snare an over-abundance of dreams. They are pretty easy to find these days, but if there are none in stores near you, a world of choices ranging from simple to elaborate versions can be found, like so much else, online.

Surrounding yourself with a bubble of light for protection, safety, and good boundaries can also be useful. Find the colors that are just right for your purpose. There are no right or wrong colors, and it can change from night to night or remain constant. White contains all the colors, but you might just as easily want green or blue or purple. Listen to what feels right to you. And, of course, you are not limited to one per night. One of my clients wrapped a full rainbow around herself and her bed nightly.

You might imagine closing a door in your mind before going to sleep. This door is to the portal between the waking world and the dreaming world. You can also add a phrase such as, "I close the door to unwanted intrusions in the night." Allow yourself to really visualize the door or portal in your mind's eye, and be sure it is well closed. You might want to imagine hearing that "click" as the door shuts. It could be a door you know from your actual life, or an imaginary one, or even your idea of a wormhole or mystic portal to the other side.

Finally, try saying the word *no* strongly, perhaps even out loud, to your dream muse. Be firm and clear that you are setting a limit and a boundary. Before going to sleep, decide if you would like a dream to come through that night. Then write a sentence or two about the issue or topic you would like guidance on, and end the writing with a seal or verbal stamp (in Hebrew this is called the *chatima*, the seal of closure on a prayer). Your closure can be "may it be so" or "just this and no more," or whatever feels right to you.

Writing down your intentions for a dream is part of the practice of dream incubation. We turn to that in a moment in chapter 3.

EXERCISE

To get better at remembering your dreams, read Appendix I before you go to bed. Prepare yourself with the tools of your trade (notebook and pen, or a phone/computer) before going to sleep, and keep them within easy reach of your bed. Pre-write the date at the top of your page. You may also decide to try a meditation before sleep that includes messages to your dreaming self that you welcome the visits and transmissions of the dream muse, and that you plan to honor them by remembering and recording the information they bring. You might say something like, "I relax into the arms of sleep safely and peacefully. I welcome messages from the night that come through to guide me in my life." Upon awakening, use the suggestions and tools from this chapter to record your dream. Please remember not to judge it or censor it, that one word is just as good as several paragraphs, and a feeling or an image is also a dream. You can write down things like "Dreamed of the color green" or "Felt anxious in the night because of dreams that I don't recall the content of" or "Had an image of a face really close to mine—that's all." One key to remembering is not to get discouraged if you don't recall dreams quickly, it just sometimes takes longer. One of these mornings you will catch a dream. This is advice I often give to myself in a variety of situations, and to all who share the quality of impatience.

Your goal at this stage is not to interpret the dream, but to pin it down so you can then work with it. If you do have immediate thoughts or associations to your dream, put them in a separate section so that they don't get confused with the dream as you truly dreamt it. Some people like to use different colored inks to record their feeling states or dream associations to differentiate them from the dream narrative itself. You can also add graphics, or doodles or art to your dream journal entries.

If you are one of the prolific dreamers who is overwhelmed by sheer volume each night, try some of the dream-containing exercises, such as hanging a dreamcatcher or writing down your intentions to only remember the dream or dreams that won't overwhelm your system. You can even specifically write your intention not to remember more than one dream a night, or whatever number seems manageable to you. If you suffer from nightmares, you can ask your dream muse to separate out the affect and the feelings from the narrative content until you have the skills and resources to effectively and safely deal with them. Put the feeling states away in a box for now; you will learn nightmare soothing and management skills in chapter 11. Or, write in your journal before sleeping that you promise your unconscious to deal with the fears or issues that generate your nightmares, so you don't need to be reminded to do so with scary dreams and try to get a break from them altogether.

Three

THE ANCIENT AND MODERN
PRACTICE OF DREAM INCUBATION

"If you will it, it is no dream."
Theodor Hertzl

Dream incubation, in a nutshell, is endeavoring to dream on purpose. In ancient times, rituals that accompanied this goal often included embarking on a journey to a sacred site, bringing sacrifices to the gods, and praying for a healing or revealing dream. In modern times, we might be more apt to take a long hot shower, light a candle, meditate, and write down the question we are hoping to get an answer to. We then go to sleep hoping to have a dream that clearly answers this question.

At its core, dream incubation is about intentionality. We intentionally turn to a source of wisdom that is larger than ourselves, and open to the response we get from the universe through the portal of our dreams. A classic definition of dream incubation by Juliette Harrison, senior lecturer at Birmingham University, in "The Classical Greek Practice of Incubation and Near Eastern Predecessors" is, "A practice in which a person performs a ritual act and then sleeps in a sacred place, with the deliberate intention of receiving a divine dream." We can either visit or create sacred space, and will return to this idea in our chapter on the landscapes of our dreams.

Dream incubation is most often used to ask for a specific dream to address an issue or problem that is important in your life, as I did when adopting our daughter. It might be a question about your health, a creative block, or a relational conundrum. Incubating a dream is a way of lining up our queries and our intentions with the highest Source to get answers, or at least guidance to questions that we are not able to fully answer on our own. Through the practice of intentional dreaming, morning can bring new light to the dilemmas we were stuck with when we went to sleep the night before.

"Sleep temples" are documented in ancient Greek, Roman, and Egyptian literature and archaeology. Dreams were respected as indicators of health, and they were seen as an opportunity for mortals to connect with the gods to gain access to their wisdom and healing. There is a long and ubiquitous tradition for incubating dreams throughout antiquity. In ancient Egypt, the god Imhotep had temples dedicated to dream healing, and in ancient Greece the god Asclepius held that post. Across time and place, dreams are honored as a resource and as a physician's guide for healing all manner of ills, both physical and spiritual.

These ancient dream temples continue to attract thousands of visitors today, many of whom have left written testimony of their healing experiences. Alfred Watkins described his experiences at these temples in his book *The Old Straight Track*. Other researchers such as Paul Devereux and Hartmann and Curry also observe that the temples were frequently built on invisible power or ley lines on the earth, which correspond with the earth's magnetic field. The geo-magnetic charges and the positive or negative ions thus charged affect our own bio-energy fields. This theory, sometimes known in America as the "Sedona Effect" after the energy vortexes that Sedona, Arizona is known for, may explain why we continue to be drawn to these sites.

Kimberly Patton of Harvard Divinity School, in her paper "Ancient Asclepia: Institutional Incubation and the Hope of Healing," writes about ancient dream incubation. In ancient Greece, pilgrims from all over the land would regularly make journeys to the temple of Asclepius, god of medicine and healing, to receive healing dreams. According to the visitworldheritage.com website, the ministry of culture and sports of Greece, and the Greek Medicine blog of David Osborn, they would bring gifts gold or silver or of cakes and honey to the priests and priestesses of the temple. Then the pilgrims would oft-times be given a "prescription" to sleep in the sacred dream temples in a special area called the abaton for the express purpose of having a healing dream. When they got to the temple, the seekers would ritually cleanse and purify themselves and set their healing intention. The supplicants would then sleep the night there under the stars, often in the company of other pilgrims seeking healing. This practice was called incubation, from the Greek word meaning "to lie upon."

Later that night, the temple priest or priestess would set small, non-venomous, yellowish-white snakes loose among the sleepers. The snakes would slither about the dreamers and were thought to whisper the healing dreams into their ears.

In the morning, if the supplicant had a dream, the priestess would help them to interpret it. Many cures were reported from this method. Asclepius himself, son of the god Apollo, was trained in healing arts by the centaur Chiron, but it was his encounter with a wise snake that apparently gave him the power even to raise the dead. His staff is depicted as entwined with snakes and is a prototype for the caduceus, the modern symbol of medicine.

Luckily for us, snakes are generally no longer part of the prescription for our own dream incubation journeys. However, other parts of the ancient ritual can be easily adapted. If we choose, we can still make a journey or pilgrimage to a place that is sacred to us, or holds special meaning, or we can even sleep out under the stars. But the key element of a pilgrimage is finding a private, undisturbed, and sanctified place where you can wake on your own time. It can even be in the privacy of your own bedroom that you create sacred space, and follow either the quick or the more extensive guidelines of the incubation process that follow.

Preparation for Dream Incubation

Dream incubation comes with preparation as well as intention. Anthropologist Kimberly Patton speaks of three elements common to the topography of incubation in ancestral times: purification, sacrifice, and pilgrimage. First we will look at how our ancestors may have done this, then how we might adapt it for ourselves.

Purification

First, some form of personal purification was part of the ritual. Bathing in a sacred pool of clear or flowing waters was common. In Jewish tradition, the ritual purification bath of the mikvah must contain some part fresh rainwater to make it "kosher," or ritually correct. Interestingly, according to Patton, tears or weeping were also frequently part of the purification process. Perhaps our salty tears were viewed as our own internal salt water cleansing, or our tears indicate that we are willing to make ourselves vulnerable and thus open to receiving insight. To be able to receive transmitted knowledge, we have to be receptive (and thus vulnerable).

The mystical branch of Judaism known as Kabbalah is based on this premise. The word *kabbalah* is from the root "l'kabel," meaning "to receive." It is received knowledge. Revered teachers in both the mystical Sufi and Kabbalistic traditions (notably Hefetz and Reb Nachman, respectively) teach that when our hearts are broken open, that is where God is able to enter.

Two of the most frequently watched TED Talks are those by Brene Brown on vulnerability. In them she normalizes and elevates this state of being, contrasting the beauty and the ultimate humanity of open-hearted vulnerability, as opposed to viewing it with shame. Connected to this concept of beauty in the brokenness is the Japanese art of *kintsugi*. This craft consists of repairing a broken piece of pottery by filling the cracks with gold or silver. Thus the repaired piece is actually more valuable than the original un-cracked piece. What a wonderful metaphor for healing: that we are the more valuable for having repaired the places where we have been cracked open than for never having been broken at all. When we purify ourselves in this part of the dream incubation process, we are letting in this beauty and healing to find the parts of ourselves that are seeking answers and responses to our deepest quests.

Sacrifice

For our ancestors, the next step to incubating a dream was having a proper frame of mind and making the proper sacrifices. For our biblical foremothers and forefathers, the sacrifices often included burnt offerings, usually of a sheep or goat. The supplicant would then sleep on the skin of the sacrificed animal. Patton tells us that the burning of the animal transformed its physical earthiness into the world of smoke and vapor and air, thus allowing the gods to smell the pleasing odor as the burnt offering went up in the smoke.

The concept of the Four Worlds of earth, air, fire, and water appears in many mystic, pagan, and indigenous traditions, as well as in Jungian typology. Therefore, a ritual that connects us with each of these worlds makes intuitive as well as logical sense. We burned the animal (fire) on the earth, it rose in smoke (air), and we purified ourselves by bathing in water.

Pilgrimage

Pilgrimage is the third step of this incubation process. This is about locality, or as the realtor says, "location, location, location." An outward journey is taken to imitate the inward journey one hopes will happen. Anthropologist James Frazer (whose classic text is *The Golden Bough*) spoke of several kinds of magical practices he found in his studies, and one of the most common was imitative magic. The pilgrimage part of dream incubation is the external manifestation of what we hope our inner dream journey will imitate. The promise of dream journeying is mimicked by where one actually sleeps, ideally in a sacred place set apart. Our ancestors would frequently travel great distances in order to incubate their dreams on holy ground.

Alternately, the ground on which the ritual took place would become holy by virtue of the Divine being accessed in that place. Frequently, holy ground, by whatever means, was in a high place—on a hill or a mound. Perhaps the membrane between the worlds of ordinary and non-ordinary reality is thinner in those spots, just as the air is thinner atop high mountains. Think of the tall standing stones of Druidic or Celtic traditions reaching up to the heavens, of Mount Sinai where Moses met God and received the Ten Commandments. Isaac had to go with Abraham, his father, "up the mountain" and climb Mount Moriah, in preparation for what could have been the ultimate sacrifice of his life. Jerusalem is ringed with seven hills, and traveling to Jerusalem is referred to as an *aliyah*, literally meaning "going up." Rome and Athens were also built on seven hills. "Castles on a hill" are often seen in fairy tales. Our fabled city of Oz is set on a hill. As Dorothy and her companions emerged from the dark forest, there it was, gleaming on the horizon. When we think about incubating dreams in the classical sense, (one that includes an external form of pilgrimage,) we can see how these high places allow us closer access to the source of dreams: the gods themselves. Even in modern times, the metaphors of "up" and "down" are used to describe holy and sacred or secular and earth-bound directions. Dreams are often envisioned as coming down to us from above. Thus our actual or metaphoric pilgrimage to the places of the gods of the dream-world has us going "up" to receive this knowledge.

Dream Incubation for Our Times

How are we to translate these ritual elements for our times, since most of us aren't about to kill a sheep or spend the night alone atop a mountain? At its root, the word *sacrifice* means to make sacred. For us, the sacred may be our quest, or intention, or our desire to connect with a higher source of wisdom. For our portion of dream wisdom, we may need to make a sacrifice of some kind, perhaps letting go of an outmoded way of thinking, or of an old belief or lifestyle. It also could be letting go of or sacrificing an easy way of doing something for the harder but ultimately healthier way. Are we willing to walk our walk, as well as talk our talk, since we may not always like the answers that we get? If you are journaling about your dream intentions and what you are incubating a dream for, you might write down your willingness to follow the guidance and wisdom from your dream muse, even if it is uncomfortable or inconvenient. For example, if you are incubating a dream on a health issue, can you make the intention or write down that you are willing to make the sacrifice to change your diet or lifestyle to support greater health? For example, to resolve some long-standing back pain, I had to sacrifice sleeping in for getting to the gym on a more regular basis. If you have a relationship dilemma, are you willing to sacrifice your own pride or ego to compromise or apologize?

To practice purification we might cleanse ourselves by smudging with sage or incense. We may decide to take a long shower or a bath with clear intention to prepare ourselves to dream deeply. We could drink a bit of salt water or wash with it as our ancestors did. We can surround ourselves with a blanket or bubble of pure white light in our mind's eye before going to sleep, or envision ourselves breathing out negativity as we prepare to sleep and dream.

Pilgrimage today can be an inner or an outer journey. We might take ourselves off on a retreat to a yoga center, or camping out in the woods to have a pilgrimage experience away from the business of our daily lives. We might set aside an hour or a day to meditate, journal, and reflect on our life and the incubating question we want to pose to our dream muse. As our ancestors sought out high places, we too may be able to find a high place from which to contemplate our questions, and thus take ourselves out of ordinary time and/or space for a bit. Breathwork techniques or meditation can take us far and deep into an inner journey.

Here are two examples of small pilgrimage/incubation journeys I took. A few years ago I felt an overload in my life, and I asked a friend if I could use her meditation room for a day. I drove to her house just twenty minutes away and spent seven hours in lovely solitude. I even had a nap with a dream in that designated space that contained within it the energies of the people who had done yoga and meditation there over many years. It later occurred to me that it was even a high place: to get to that room I had to climb up a crawl ladder to the finished attic that served as the meditation space.

Sometimes we don't know that a spot is holy to us until we have had a liminal experience in it. Our patriarch Jacob did not know before his dream nap on the stone (where he had his dream of the angels ascending and descending from heaven on a ladder) that this was a holy place. He later named the spot Beit El, meaning House of God.

For my second pilgrimage, in order to have the time and quiet to begin to turn five years of short blog posts into a book about dreams, I went off by myself on a solo writing retreat for four days. I was not atop a mountain, nor did I sacrifice a goat, but instead rented a small cottage on a lake in Western Massachusetts. As a busy professional and mom, I relished answering solely to my own rhythms for a few days. I had my purification waters with the lake at my doorstep, and I sacrificed television, internet access, and indoor heating during that time.

On my second day there I received a gift: at 10 a.m. I sighted a large barred owl right above my head as I walked in the woods. Mornings are not the time an owl is usually about. Nocturnal creatures, they are more often spotted after dark. It felt like a sign that my dream muse, taking the form of this night owl, showed up during the day and was blessing this time and space as an answer to my dreams.

The Core of Dream Incubation Today

The core of the practice of dream incubation is to simply spend a few quiet moments before going to sleep to write down in your dream journal the question, the dilemma, or the issue that you would like some guidance on. Take a few minutes, or longer if you choose, for this writing process, but try to end up with a specific question. The more specific your question, the easier it will be to see how it is answered in the dream. That was the only thing I did before incubating the dream to bring our daughter home, but my intention was extremely strong—I needed that answer.

Be sure to date your writings as well, as it may take more than one night for a reply to come through. It can often take several days of intentional dreaming on the same question to get your answer. You may need to reframe or clarify your question before you get a dream in response.

You can also spend a little time on the purification part of the ritual by bathing yourself or cleaning your room to prepare a sacred space. A saltwater bath and lighting a candle or incense can help to clear out the energetic space for answers to come through.

Joy, a member of my dream circle, found a lovely variation on this method. She had several important dreams involving whales over the years, and felt that she gained much valuable information from the whales in her dreams. She began to use them as her guides, and now incubates dreams by directing her queries to her "Whale Council" when she has a dilemma she wants to dream on.

Before going to sleep, you can align your dreaming mind with the wisdom of the universe with the simple steps stated above. When you wake, write down the dream on the same page that you wrote your question, even if it is not clear to you how the dream applies. Later, when you work with the dream you received, you can see on the same page exactly what question you were asking and how the dream connected to it. Often the connections appear later on, so don't despair if you can't figure it out right away.

EXERCISE

Think of a dilemma or question you have in your life today. It may be something fairly straightforward, such as choosing the best place to have your next vacation, or as life-changing as deciding whether or not to marry the person you are dating. Decide if the pilgrimage part of the ritual speaks to you, or if sleeping well in your own bed is just right. If a pilgrimage speaks to you, you can sit for a few minutes by your local pond, hike in a nearby woods, or visit a place of worship or any spot that feels sacred to you. Find what feels right. If there is something you need to give up, to sacrifice in order to get what you want, spend some time thinking about that. It might be something concrete, like sugar, or something ephemeral like time or convenience.

Finally, decide if you want to do any preparation of yourself or your surroundings for the purification part of the ceremony. If so, you can take a saltwater bath, visit the ocean, or smudge with sage before writing and sleeping, then spend some time outlining the problem in your dream journal. Be sure to end your writing with a question that is as specific as possible. Set your intention, turn off the lights, and sleep.

Remember that dream responses and answers often come through in symbols and images that you will then have to decode. Therefore, after you have dreamed your dream and written it down with as many details as you can, look for associations, metaphors, analogies, puns, and plays on words. If you are not able to decode the message, ask your dreaming friends, aka your dream "posse," for some help. If you cannot get clarity, ask for another dream to explain the first one, maybe trying my bossy stance to ask for it to come to you this time in clear, unambiguous language!

Four
....

THE NATURE OF DREAMS: DREAMING
WHILE ASLEEP AND AWAKE

"We are such stuff that dreams are made on,
and our little life is rounded by sleep."
William Shakespeare, The Tempest

As we dream, we create worlds apart. We remember things we barely knew, or "re-member" the pieces together from our unconscious pool of wisdom. We embark on mythic and soul-stirring journeys, make meaning out of metaphor, and weave gossamer strands of silk and stars in our nightly sojourns. As we learned in chapter 1 on dreaming across cultures, the Aboriginal peoples of Australia hold that the dreamtime is what brought the world into being.

Dreams as Alternate Reality

The energy portal of the dream state swings back and forth between what we call ordinary reality and non-ordinary reality. There are three types of dreams: sleep dreams, waking dream states (such as intuition, synchronicity, and déjà vu), and daydreams.

What we call daydreams are not quite dream states per se, as much as they are a type of reverie. Our mind is off on its own, so to speak, untethered from our current surroundings. Daydreaming, also called mind-wandering, most commonly refers to musing, spacing out, or wool gathering as we drift off to somewhere other than our present surroundings. During a daydream, we are caught up in our own internal thoughts or fantasies, such as, "What should I have for dinner?" or "Wasn't that last vacation at the beach so lovely..." rather than attending to whatever is happening in our actual environment (such as math class, our board meeting, or a conversation with our child).

What these three dream states do have in common, though, is some kind of link to non-ordinary reality or an altered connection to time and space. Each gives us access to information that is not available to our ordinary left-brain linear thinking, and/or allows us to somehow be two places at once. We can be in our own bed at night and at the same time be on safari in the jungle. We can be sitting in math class and simultaneously be on the beach where we spent our last vacation, as we review it in the form of memory. We can run into a person or situation and have the distinct feeling that we are reliving something that has happened to us before in another time or place (the experience of déjà vu). Knowing from the relatively new field of neuroscience research that we currently understand only a small part of how our brains work, it stands to reason that the rest of our mysterious grey matter has additional abilities and functions. We just don't fully understand how to recognize, control, or quantify these other states or functions—yet. Linear thinking is not the only valid form of information gathering.

Shamans and mystics from cultures throughout the world speak to us of the dream world as a very real place, a parallel universe if you will. Many spiritual traditions believe that our soul can leave our bodies at night during a dream and travel in the astral realms. This, by the way, is the reason you are not supposed to wake a sleeper up too suddenly. Several mystical traditions describe the dreaming soul as connected to the body by a thin silver thread, and awakening too suddenly can snap the thread leaving the soul unable to find its way home back to the body.

Lynn McTaggert, in her landmark book on non-local consciousness, *The Field,* writes: "Deep in the rainforests of the Amazon, the Achur and the Huaorani Indians are assembled for their daily ritual … At dawn … as the world explodes into light, they share their dreams … The dreamer is the vessel the dream decided to borrow to have a conversation with the whole tribe."

For these tribes, the dream is not an individual possession; it is owned collectively. I love that phrase: "The dreamer is the vessel that the dream decided to borrow." Doesn't it feel like that at times? That we are but the vessel when we wake with the sense that something came *through* us, rather than *from* us? My friend's daughter, Talia, created the lovely word *blessel* when she was young, combining the words blessing and vessel. So when we have powerful dreams for ourselves or for our tribe, we function as a blessel too.

Michael Harner, anthropologist and shamanic practitioner, remarks that one of the core principles of shamanism is that spirits are real, and that spirits produce dreams. Shamanic theory proposes that the human soul and other spirits that have formed an attachment to a person can produce their dreams. While we have no way to verify this, I instinctively resonate with this idea. It is one way of understanding those vivid visitation dreams we sometimes get of departed loved ones—that their spirits still have an attachment to us and thus visit to provide comfort or just to say, "Hi, we still are here with you." That is an infinitely reassuring thought to me.

The shamanic concept that dreams can facilitate the bond between souls that have spent time together while living in their bodies feels like another type of homecoming. Through our dreams, we are always coming home to our truest and most authentic selves, and also potentially to the other souls we have traveled through life with.

Here is another viewpoint on the source of our dreams. The Greek philosopher Philo tells us that there are three ways to understand our nighttime dreams: there are those that originate within us, those that originate in the angelic or spirit realm, and those that originate with God. Our prophets and holy men and women frequently report conversations with God or angels either in a dream, or as a waking dream day-vision. In Philo's view, some of our dreams are human-sized and some are angel- or God-sized.

What Else Is a Dream?

The origin of the word *dream* in the English language is from the Middle English *dreem* (1050), which originally meant joy, mirth, and gladness. A more current definition of *dream* by blogger Daniel Aolaya is "a visionary creation of the imagination."

We use the word *dream* to mean many things today. It can mean wishful thinking: "I can only dream of that." Related, but slightly different is a dream as something you aspire to: "My dream job would be …" Realizing these ambitions and satisfying a wish are also referred to as a "dream come true."

On the other side of the spectrum, the word *dream* is also used to refer to bunk, garbage, or a waste of time, as in "It's only a pipe dream." There is the whole concept of "broken dreams." In this more negative category is the concept of dreaming as being unrealistic, or suffering delusions.

It is fascinating to me that the same word is used to refer to such opposite concepts and ideas. We seem to have a complicated relationship with our dreams. If someone is *living in a dream world*, is that a positive or negative thing? (I guess it depends on if you can still pay your bills on time). The words *dream* and *hallucination* are sometimes used interchangeably.

Then we have a love object—"He's so dreamy"—or something that works very well and smoothly—"It runs like a dream." When we imagine something that may be beyond our present reach, we say, "You're just dreaming." On the contrary, when there is something we could not imagine doing, we say, "I wouldn't dream of it." We are clearly besotted with this multifaceted word, and use it to represent a wide variety of feelings, ideas, opinions, and states of consciousness.

Our minds and our bodies provide us with information through our dreams. We are multifaceted beings: logical and imaginative, made of clay and made of stardust. Dr. Patrick McNamara, a neuroscientist at Boston University School of Medicine, encourages doctors to routinely ask patients about their dreams as a way of assessing mental status. "Dreams are faithful reports of a patient's emotional life," he states. Unresolved emotional baggage from days or decades ago can show up in our dreams, trying desperately to get our attention by keeping alive the memories and feelings connected to the events until such time as we are able to sufficiently resolve them. This is also the essence of PTSD dreaming: replaying prior traumas in real or symbolic fashion in our dreams. The chapter on nightmares provides tools for soothing, containing, and working through traumatic dreams to achieve greater peace.

Prodromal dreams are our medic alert dreams. I have encountered countless stories in the dream-sharing world of men and women who have had recurring dreams pointing to something being awry in their bodies, even though they had no symptoms to report. The dreams are frequently symbolic in nature rather than literal, so in this line of inquiry it is important to get consultation from others. Some people use their dreams to accelerate their healing by using incubation, dream re-entry techniques, and other dreamwork methods. One key line of questioning when working on a dream is to ask whether the dream might be pointing to a physical symptom that needs some attention. If we get an "aha" reaction, then the next step might be a doctor's appointment to follow up on these clues.

The Neuroscience of a Dream

Imaging studies at Harvard University, through NIH (the National Institutes of Health) and studied by Drs. David Kahn, Robert Stickgold, Allan Hobson and others, have shown that our brains do not discriminate between waking and sleeping realities. As far as our brains are concerned, the events and imagery in our dreams are the same as the events and imagery in our waking lives. I love that discovery. It confirms, in a sense, what our shamans and mystics have been telling us. Here's how it works.

(Warning: I am something of a neuroscience geek, so this next part is a bit technical.)

To start with, there are two sides to your brain. While there is overlap, the left side of your brain provides the majority of logical, linear, and sequential thinking, while the right side of your brain contributes to most of your creativity, imagination, and intuition. These two sides are divided by what looks like a seam in pictures, called the corpus callosum. You also have front, center, and back parts to your brains. The front part, right behind your forehead, is the cortex. This is where most of your declarative thinking and parts of your memory is stored. At the back of your head, just above your neck, is the medulla, which controls most of your autonomic systems such as respiration and digestion. Deep inside the center of the brain is your limbic system, which holds court with your emotional world, contains the unconscious parts of memory, and provides both the accelerator (the amygdala) and the brakes (the hippocampus) when you perceive threat or danger. This is where the flight, fight, and freeze responses are generated.

Neuroimaging studies show that dreams emerge from multiple parts of our brains, including the limbic system and the orbital-frontal cortex, which is the visual and social center of our cortex located right behind our eyes. Harvard neuroscientist Dr. David Kahn informed me that dreams "have amazing complexity" because they involve many areas of the brain at once. "The limbic system helps to account for the emotionality of our dreams, and the orbital-frontal cortex helps account for the social nature of dreams and for the interactions between the dream self with others in the dream."

Both the limbic system and the cortex are structures that straddle the central seam of the corpus callosum. Thus they are found on both sides of the brain. This may be why dreams do not discriminate between waking and sleeping realities. Because our dreams are generated from both sides of our brains, they gain content and traction from both parts and functions. Once again we see the capacity of dreams to link more than one world at a time, here examined in a physiological structural sense. Stay tuned, we're almost there.

When we awake we recall and work on our dreams using our prefrontal cortex (the area under our foreheads), which holds our thinking and declarative memory. Finally, connecting the dots between our night *experience* of dreaming and our daytime *memory* of the dream is the medial temporal lobe, the part of the brain that serves as a bridge between memories and visual recognition, and helps us process things that we've seen and that have happened to us.

Here's the punch line. Neuroscience has also figured out why our eyes move (REM) while we are dreaming. Researchers Nir and Fried, in the *Nature Communications Journal,* noticed that each flicker of our eyes accompanies a new image in our dream, with the eye movements "essentially acting like a reset function between individual dream image 'snapshots.' By using electrodes that had been implanted in patients' brains prior to brain surgery to alleviate epileptic seizures, they found that '*the neural brain activity while seeing new images in a dream was essentially the same as when actually seeing new images in waking life*' (author's italics)." In other words, neuroscience confirms that the brain does not distinguish between the waking sights and the dream images. No wonder our dream adventures and characters seem so real— to our dreaming brains, they truly are!

Now, as a palate cleanser for your left brain, a bit of dream poetry sorbet for your right brain:

Last Night as I Was Sleeping
By Antonio Machado (translated by Robert Bly)

Last night as I was sleeping,
I dreamt—marvelous error!—
that a spring was breaking
out in my heart.
I said: Along which secret aqueduct,
Oh water, are you coming to me,
water of a new life
that I have never drunk?

Last night as I was sleeping,
I dreamt—marvelous error!—
that I had a beehive
here inside my heart.
And the golden bees
were making white combs
and sweet honey
from my old failures.

Last night as I was sleeping,
I dreamt—marvelous error!—
that a fiery sun was giving
light inside my heart.
It was fiery because I felt
warmth as from a hearth,
and sun because it gave light
and brought tears to my eyes.

Last night as I slept,
I dreamt—marvelous error!—

that it was God I had
here inside my heart.

Synchronicities and Intuition:
Our Waking Dream States

Synchronicity, a term coined by Carl Jung in *Synchronicity: An Acausal Connecting Principle,* is defined as "the experience of two or more events that seem unrelated or unlikely to occur together by chance, yet are experienced as occurring together in a meaningful manner." Synchronistic events serve to reveal underlying patterns and a larger conceptual framework. We accidentally stumble into this world at times. When we do, if we stop and tune in, more of the patterns in life will be revealed to us. We are given a glimpse of an order larger than ourselves.

Synchronicities call us up short and take our breath away. We are more likely to encounter this threshold between worlds when we are looking for and paying attention to the potential for meaningful messages in our lives, but this liminal space can also show up unasked. It is the world of meaningful coincidences. "Co-incidences" refers to things that are "co-occurring," the kind of phenomenon that prompt us to say something like, "Wow. What are the odds that I should run into you here, of all places?" or "I just was talking to Joe about how long it has been since we've been in touch when you called me." Or even, what are the odds that I should see a night owl at 10 a.m. just as I am writing a book about dreams?

Meaningful coincidences or synchronicities are found in the realm of the waking dream-weave of strange co-occurrences; the experience of déjà vu; in unusual meetings and "out of the blue" connections and happenings. Some of them are fun, some are uncanny, and some are awe-inspiring. The uncanny quality of this seeing and knowing is connected to our ability to "dream while awake"; that is, to access other ways and other planes of knowing. It allows us to connect with Spirit and to be refreshed by it. What may seem to be accidental coincidences may actually be signals from the universe that something we seek is right here, or that something here is seeking us. Being awake to our sleeping and waking dreams allows us to find meanings and patterns that can enrich our lives.

Here is a three-part example of synchronicity. Part 1: I am working with my client Susan one night, and we are talking about the foxes that have shown up in her dreams several times in the last week. Part 2: A few hours later I have a message from her on my voicemail, where she excitedly informs me, "I had to tell you that a fox just crossed the street in front of my car as I was pulling up to my driveway—and I've never seen one here before." Here was synchronistic confirmation of the importance of the "fox medicine" for her life.

Part 3: This part of the fox story ties together synchronicity and intuition. Susan's dream foxes came as an response to an issue she had been working on in therapy, "Why do I tend to push people away when I begin to get close to them, and why do I quickly lose my trust in people for minor infractions?" Exploring her childhood history of abandonment and neglect provided her with some insight into this pattern. Then the foxes appeared both in her night dreams and again through an actual living encounter. We didn't yet know how they were related to this issue, but acknowledged that when something is doubled in our sleeping or our waking dream life it is a sign of importance.

Here's where intuition comes in. The following week, while working with Susan on her dream of the foxes, for no apparent reason I had a strong recall of the book *The Little Prince*, and of the fox in that story. This book is an allegory about loneliness and the need for trust in order to have relationships, as told through the eyes of a little prince who lands on earth from another planet. The fox he meets in the story teaches the little prince that the most important things in life are visible only to the heart, and that it is his love for his rosebush on his home planet that makes the bush unique and worth caring for.

I have learned over the years that when I get an association to someone else's dream I should pay attention to it and offer it, but not to impose it on them (remembering that the dream belongs to the dreamer). I do, however, want to be sure to check in to see if it may have any relevance for them. This is part of the power of dream-sharing with others—we all have the power to tap into associations that the dreamer may not have considered yet and that are present in what Jung identifies as our collective unconscious.

I asked Susan, "Are you familiar with this story?" and she replied, "It is one of my favorite books from childhood." So there was a hit already. She remembered the fox, but not its significance. We reviewed that part of the story, recalling that the fox taught the little prince how to tame him. I then pulled the book off my shelf and we read together: Each day the fox comes a little closer and closer until he finally lets the prince sit next to him and pet him. Then after some time the fox tells the little prince he has to leave. "But why?" asks the little prince, "I shall cry if you leave." The fox replies, "One runs the risk of weeping a little if one lets oneself be tamed." The price of closeness and intimacy is a willingness to be vulnerable, a willingness to take the risk.

The dream foxes and the fox in her driveway and the fox from the Little Prince all came to share this message with her: letting people get close and trusting them does not guarantee that they will never leave, but taking that risk is often worth the price. For you never know, if you let them get close, they just might stay. And even if they don't, as with the fox in *The Little Prince*, the encounter is still a treasure and that can be held forever in the memory of your heart. Susan took this message to her own heart as she began to tiptoe toward more trust and connections in her life. Had Susan not been paying attention to the possibility of a response to her questions, she would have missed the importance of those foxes.

Another example of synchronicity occurred while I was at a dream conference in Berkeley, California. I was walking along the marina and was talking with a colleague about the quote from Chinese Taoist philosopher Zhuangzi in *The Butterfly as Companion*, "Once upon a time, I dreamt I was a butterfly, fluttering hither and thither, to all intents and purposes a butterfly. I was conscious only of my happiness as a butterfly, unaware that I was myself. Soon I awaked, and there I was, veritably myself again. Now I do not know whether I was then a man dreaming I was a butterfly, or whether I am now a butterfly, dreaming I am a man."

As we spoke a large black and yellow swallowtail butterfly flew over our heads, circled us a few times, and then landed on the flowering bush next to us. It stopped us in our tracks. The next day I attended a workshop about dream traditions in Bali, and the presenter told us that she had asked the local shaman while she was there, "What is the best possible dream that a Balinese person could have?" His reply was "To dream of a butterfly on a flower." When I told the presenter about my encounter, her response was "I think that you received a blessing," which is exactly how I felt.

Nonlinear Time

The poets and the mystics have always known that there is more to our world than we can measure, and that time can move forward and backward and even stand still. (For example, we are told that the sun stood still when Joshua blew his horn over Jericho). Rabbi Alan Ullman teaches that we inhabit sacred time when we are aware that the past, the present, and the future are all simultaneously existing.

Lewis Carroll provides us with a humorous look at the construct of time. The White Queen tells Alice in *Through the Looking Glass* that it was possible to live both forward and backward in time. The Queen told Alice that the advantage of this is that one's memory then works in both ways. Alice responded that she never heard of such a thing, that she was sure her memory only worked one way and she couldn't remember things before they happened. The Queen then replied "It's a poor sort of memory that only works backwards."

Quantum physicists have been in the process of working on proving Einstein's theory of relativity for years. There really does seem to be a "time-space continuum" that is not solely the province of science fiction or Star Trek. Jung himself felt there was a connection between relativity and quantum physics, and scientists are now confirming that our intuitions about the potential realities of time travel and non-local consciousness are actually scientifically valid.

In July of 2012, the Boston Globe reported on their front page that on the fourth of July, Independence Day, the world of quantum physics announced that researchers had finally found the Higgs boson particle, or what they colloquially are calling the "God particle." No wonder it was front-page news! This discovery has to do with uncovering intrinsic patterns of symmetry in nature and the finding that all matter, even weightless matter, has mass. They report that everything in nature is part of a pattern, and that even things that have no weight still have mass and take up space. That implies that our very thoughts, nay, our dreams, have weight and patterns and mass as well. This discovery of a new particle might hold a key to understanding the nature of the universe. Years ago, philosopher Pierre Teilhard de Chardin in *The Phenomenon of Man* wrote, "Matter is spirit moving slowly enough to be seen."

Patterns in nature and in dreams are just what we have been talking about. It makes synchronicity seem almost matter of fact. It confirms the point that the line between dreams and "reality" is very fine indeed. When everything in nature is part of a pattern, then the implication is that the pattern extends into the past and the future as well. Our dreaming mind has this ability to transcend time and space, retrieving information from both the past and the possible future, and keeping us connected to Rabbi Ullman's sacred time, in which we simultaneously stand in the past, the present, and the future all at once.

Intuition, Dreams, and Peeking into the Possible Future

Dreams and intuition are connected. Precognitive dreaming means that we dream something that later occurs in waking life. In essence, intuition is about the ability to see around corners into a future time. We have to remember our dreams to know if they come to pass; this is another reason why writing them down becomes crucial. It is highly likely that many of us experience precognitive dreams regularly; we just don't remember them.

Not all precognitive dreaming is earth shattering. It can be about the mundane events of our everyday lives, such as "I dreamed that it was going to be pouring rain next Monday when it was my turn to drive carpool"—and then it is. Hopefully our precognitions are not like those of poor Cassandra of Greek mythology. She was a powerful seer, but she only had the ability to foretell disaster. People tended to run in the opposite direction when they saw her coming. Additionally, the waking dream state of déjà vu, that "I've been here before" feeling, may be the echo of a forgotten dream. The term *déjà vu* itself is French for "already seen," and is the overwhelming feeling of familiarity with something that we have no recollection of having actually experienced before.

Moving now from precognition to intuition, author and energy worker Anodea Judith in *Eastern Body, Western Mind* writes, "Intuition is a leap toward wholeness from fragmentation." A strong intuitive closely attends to their inner promptings and to their dreams as well as to their outer surroundings. To purposefully access our intuition, we need to set our intention, then ask the right questions, and finally listen and watch for the answers (notice that we must both listen and look since we don't know what form the answer might arrive in). One time, in response to a question I was holding in my mind about how to enhance a relationship, I got a message from a large billboard for a hairdressing salon: it told me to have "serious fun." You never know where the response may show up! Be sure to be on the lookout for puns and plays on words—the universe can be a jokester at times.

It is easy to miss this third step of listening and watching once the question is asked. As well as watching and listening for signs, we might also experience the response as a synesthesia, a state of being where our senses mingle and we see sounds, or taste sights.

To complete the loop with intuitive ways of knowing, we also need to learn how to listen both from the inside and from the outside, just like dreamwork. When we work on our dreams, we can do so from outside the dream, by processing and analyzing what we have dreamt, or from the inside, whereby we re-enter the dream in our waking imagination, and re-experience it in present time.

To receive wisdom from your intuition, listen to the words that come to your inner ear, as well as to the emotions you feel and the body sensations you experience. All are forms of communication. Although the information that comes through may seem spontaneous, intuitive skills are frequently the accumulation of years of work and preparation in many practices that may include dreamwork, meditation, shamanic studies, mindfulness, spirituality, book learning, and tuning into subtle body signs such as a spontaneous breath, a change in temperature, or that tingle we speak about when a dream association hits home. Accessing our intuition necessitates our willingness to be open to receiving knowledge from uncanny sources asleep or awake.

When intuition comes through from our dreams in the hushed quiet of the night, it is often easier to hear that still small voice. There is no dream too small, no fragment too meaningless, nothing that we aren't able to mine some gold from. Here's an example. When my daughter's twenty-five-year-old friend died after falling while hiking alone in the mountains of Arizona, we were all bereft. A few days later I woke at 3:00 a.m. with the single word command "write" coming through from my dream. I obeyed, got up, and sat at my computer, and the poem "Song of Grief" emerged, which we read at his funeral.

Physicists are telling us that there are patterns in the universe. Energy worker Judith tells us that intuition is the unconscious recognition of patterns. She cites Satprem from *Sri Aurobindo or*

The Adventure in Consciousness describing intuition as "the flash of a match in the darkness." She expands on this, saying that for a brief moment, the whole room comes to light. We can suddenly see "the furniture, the wallpaper, the people in the room, and maybe even what is going on outside the window. And then it is gone. The match burns out. Do we remember what we have seen?"

Our ancestors were very clear that intuition was a valid form of acquiring information. We modern people are starting to do a little better at paying attention to this form of paying attention. Looking at current titles in the spirituality, psychology, and anthropology sections of a bookstore allows us to see how interested we have become in exploring this topic.

Solomon receives his portion of wisdom and earns his right to be known as "Solomon the Wise" by hearing God ask him in a dream what he most desires. He responds to that question by replying, "A Lev Shomea," which translates to "a listening heart." What a nice definition of the ability to receive wisdom from many sources—to have a listening heart. Perhaps that is the core of the intuitive process—to have a listening mind, a listening body, and a listening heart. Then we too may receive our additional portion of wisdom.

Whether our nighttime or waking dreams come from within our brains, the spirit realm, the Divine, or are mysterious patterns in the fabric of the universe, the worlds we visit on these journeys have gifts and messages for us, for our communities, and perhaps for the world. Awaken to your dreams! Use their messages to heal, to grow, to explore, to journey, and to connect with all manner of strange and wondrous beings. Go down the rabbit hole and over the rainbow to see what you may find.

Having seen that dreams are multifaceted and multi-dimensional, let us now turn to the multiple layers of meaning to be found within each dream.

EXERCISE

Develop your intuitive capacity to find meaning and messages in your waking dream states. One way to do so is similar to dream incubation, but done while awake. Put your attention on a question or a dilemma you have, and then hold it in your mind's eye as you go about your day. Every so often, take it out, literally or figuratively, and look gently at the question, asking the universe to give you a sign that will answer it. Be on the lookout throughout the day for any unusual sights, sounds, words, people, or animals that may be relevant to your question. It may be a repeating color, or song lyric, or an animal that catches your attention over and over, or is seen in unusual places.

If, for example, you are looking for confirmation about whether or not to move to another city to take a new job or go to graduate school, look for signs that seem to point one way or the other. If the job is in Denver and graduate school is in Maryland, what shows up on your radar screen? Does the song "Rocky Mountain High" come on the radio, or does your friend invite you out for Maryland-style soft shell crabs that night? By holding the question in your mind, you will begin to make connections and see patterns that you may not have noticed before. Remember that the messages can come from surprising sources (such as my billboard), and can be fun as well as serious.

Patterns are another thing that that you can be on the lookout for. You may start seeing a pattern emerge before you know what it is about, or why you are seeing or hearing these things. My client and I had foxes show up three times before we figured out the message they were bringing. The patterns can be both in your waking and your dreaming life. Held together and noticed, they can give you needed information. The combination of repetitive dreams and/or running across something over and over in waking life can be messages from both realms on the same topic. It may be the same sign, or a related one. Are you dreaming of missing phone calls, someone leaving you garbled messages, and having your power go out? And then in your waking life drop your phone in the toilet, have an argument with your partner where you can't seem to understand each other, and have an actual power failure during a storm? Taken separately, these may not seem significant, but taken all together there may be a message for your life about improving lines of communication.

Five

DREAM LAYERS: A KABBALAH-BASED METHOD OF DREAMWORK

"When we dream, we do so in improbable
layers, in unique labyrinths, in palimpsests of
experience, memory, and wishes melded into
ephemeral reality by our subconscious."
Zoe Madonna, Boston Globe, 2/12/17)

Now that we have explored several aspects of the world of the dream, we can turn our attention to the layers of meaning in our nighttime productions. As we begin to uncover the meaning of our dreams (which, to be perfectly honest, is probably what we are most interested in—"What does it mean?"), we need to realize that there is not just a single meaning. Each dream, even the simplest one, has multiple layers of information to share with us. This key concept itself will help you to get the most from your dreamwork. The longer we sit with and work with the images and the narrative, the more juice we are able to squeeze out of it.

Have you ever tried to squeeze a lemon that has just come out of the refrigerator? You can get some juice out, but it usually doesn't release all of its tart potential until it has been sitting at room temperature for a while. Try going back to it an hour or so later; you will be amazed at how much more juice is still in there. It also works to roll the lemon around a bit—that releases the juice as well. It's like that with dreams too: we have to sit with them for a while, perhaps roll them around, let them thaw out a bit, and then we can squeeze out more dream juice. All of the layers of meaning don't emerge at once; some gradually emerge over time.

We often do not have infinite time to sit and ponder or to consult with others about our dreams, so we let ourselves be satisfied with our first hits or associations. "Oh, I had pizza for dinner last night, so that's why I dreamed of pizza." Or perhaps you catch the next slightly less literal layer: "Pizza is associated with Italy for me, and I am planning a trip to Italy soon."

These meanings and associations may be quite true, but they don't quite explain why of all the things you ate yesterday or of all the possible associations to Italy you might have, pizza is the thing that showed up in your dream. Noted dream expert Jeremy Taylor in his classic book *When People Fly and Rivers Run Uphill* reminded us that no dream comes to simply tell us something that we already know. So if you work on your dream and come up solely with things that you already knew in your waking life, then you can be pretty sure that you have not received its full meaning or message. There's more there than meets the eye at first glance.

To aid in extracting more meaning out of your dreams, I developed a system that organizes the process of examining the multiple layers of a dream. It is comprised of four layers and is based on a Kabbalistic system of reading the Bible or the Torah. By using this system you can assess which layer you are working with, and determine whether you care to move on to additional layers. Here's how I developed it.

After our adoption process began, I was preparing physically as well as emotionally for this big life transition. I knew that parenting required stamina, so I upped my workouts at the gym. While on the treadmill, I listened to CDs to pass the time. One set was on the Kabbalah, and the other set was on dreamwork. I alternated days depending on my mood. What I believe happened was a crisscross of the neural networks in my brain, which consequently blended these two concepts while combined with the right, left, right, left motion on the treadmill. Dreams and Kabbalah, layers of dreams and layers of reading the Torah all blended in my mind-sight to form this system.

The PARDES System of Kabbalah:
Harvesting from the Orchard of Dreams

In Kabbalah there is a four-tiered blueprint for reading a sacred text. It is used to understand the deepest layers at which the Torah may be read. It's called the "PARDES" system—the word *pardes* itself means "orchard" in Hebrew. Simultaneously, the word is also an allegory for the Garden of Eden. The four letters that correspond in Hebrew to P, R, D, and S also form an acronym. Each letter stands for another word: P for the word *P'shat*, which means simple or literal; R for *Remez*, meaning hint; D for *Drash*, which means expounded upon; and S for *Sod*, meaning secret or hidden. We see that the word *PARDES* itself has three layers: the literal translation, an allegory, and an acronym.

When reading the Torah, the *P'shat*—the simple or literal layer—is the words themselves and the overt story as they are written down in the text. The *Remez* is the second level of understanding that we reach as we begin to grapple with the underlying meanings of the words that are written. Think of it like reading a poem: First we simply read the words the poet has written, and then we get to our own associations that are not contained in the written words themselves. This helps to deepen our appreciation of the poem.

The next layer, *Drash* comes from the root of the Hebrew word *Lidrosh*, which means to pursue, or chase after. This is the layer that is revealed to us as we plumb the depths of the text. At this layer of inquiry we might pursue the deeper meanings inside the text. Here we might examine metaphor, rhyme and rhythm, word choice, and the use of spacing between words. We might observe where else in the text this word or sentence is repeated and what might be the connection between how it is used here and how it is used in another chapter.

In the *Drash* layer, we can look at multiple meanings of the same word. As an example, we can use the word *run* in English. Depending on context, it can mean a very fast paced locomotion, or a flaw in a stocking, or ink that was wet and has leaked, or a sentence that goes on and on—a "run-on" sentence. This layer can also contain puns or plays on words. In short, anything that can take us beyond the literal to the symbolic, to associations and connections that help us weave the whole text together. And finally, the layer of *Sod*, which is literally translated as "secret," is the layer of Torah that holds mystery, mystical thought, a glimpse of divinity, and connection to worlds beyond.

When dreams are explored using this system, each level may be understood and appreciated on its own. But when all four levels are explored, the dreamer can receive insight about their past, present, and future. The dream can inform us not only about our current life projects, issues, or stuck places, but also give us information about how our past may still be helping or haunting us. At the deepest levels, the dream may give us a peek around the corner of time into possible futures or precognitions, or give us spiritual connections for ourselves and for our community. The ability to recognize this spiritual layer in our own dreams does not come easily. It seems to become more readily apparent when dreamers explore their dreams with others, who can then lend their extra eyes and ears to the dream (two or more heads being better than one). However, the strong dreamers and the shamans among us may be able to capture this layer on their own.

Using the PARDES System in Dreamwork

The following outline describes the four levels of the PARDES system as applied to dreamwork. It will be followed by several examples to further clarify how to use this system.

1. Level 1: P'shat (Simple)

This is the baseline or literal level, the story that is spelled out by the dream narrative itself. It contains the dream landscape and characters as they appear in the dream. What you see is what you get here. Your dream can be enjoyed and explored completely on the level of the dream narrative itself, without interpretive or associative elements. The content at this level can be looked at from the outside (I'm telling you my dream in the third person as I remember it) or from the inside (I'm telling my dream from inside of the story, in the first person, as if it is currently happening and I am experiencing it right now). It is not added to, changed, or interpreted, but simply journeyed through and appreciated for what it is. This is the dream's story, which you can enjoy on its own merit. For example, Joy, a member of my dream group who is an author of children's books, tells us that she frequently gets her themes and opening storylines directly from the dreams she has, sometimes full blown and ready for print.

2. Level 2: Remez (Hinted At)

This level contains our first mind and body associations to the dream material. These impressions are not necessarily contained directly in the narrative of the dream itself, as they are in the first layer. Here, as you begin to ponder the meaning of the dream, they begin to jump out at you: they have been "hinted at" by the dream material. This is the "Oh, I know what that means/symbolizes" layer. It may contain influences from things that happened in your life yesterday or recently, and these events in your life show up only slightly disguised or encoded in symbolism. "I saw Teresa yesterday; that's why she appeared in my dream," or just slightly more symbolic, "The screaming man in my dream reminds me of my father."

We can see beneath this veil fairly quickly, for the meaning is embedded just below the surface of the words and dreamscape itself. Our response to this exploration may be cognitive ("Oh, I get it"), or it may be an emotional or physical reaction. We might get hot, or anxious, or a sudden stomachache. We might feel giddy, or a tingling in our fingers, but may not yet know why. This is part of the embodied aspect of the integrated dreamwork method: What bodily responses do we have to the dream? There is plenty to work and play with at this layer of the dream.

3. Level 3: Drash (Pursued or Revealed)

The third layer of the dream to explore is *Drash*. This is the layer that is "revealed" to us when we "pursue" the dream (*Lidrosh*, the root of *Drash,* means chase or pursue). Here we will most likely use a variety of dreamwork techniques that allow us to go beyond what we know consciously or have initially associated. We often must "pursue" these meanings to uncover the true gifts of the dream.

This is the most symbolized layer. It is the layer of insight, of correlation, of deeper associations. It is where we unravel the threads of the dream. At this layer we may pursue associations that may not have even been contained in the original dream itself, but that the work on the dream material has pointed us toward. We then follow these threads emanating out from the dream to wherever they may lead us, and then back again to the connections with the original dream.

In the Greek legend of the labyrinth and the Minotaur, Princess Ariadne instructed the Athenian hero Theseus to unravel a ball of twine as he entered the labyrinth, and then to rewind it to follow it back out again. She advised this so that he would not become lost inside the labyrinth and be devoured by the Minotaur lurking in its center, as so many other young men and women had been. Like Theseus, we go deeper into the dream. We follow the threads into, and then back out of our dream. By weaving together our associations and metaphors, our personal and universal symbols, myth and fairy tale connections, and puns or plays on words, we can find ourselves inside the deep meanings of our dream. We then follow the threads and journey back out again so that we can use our discoveries to enhance our lives.

Somewhere between this layer of the work and the next one we also may encounter our shadow side. This Jungian term refers to the darker, dangerous, or unusual beings in our dream that may be showing us some hidden aspect of ourselves. They may also be showing us the exiled parts of ourselves that we may have distanced ourselves from due to embarrassment, or prefer not to recognize or own as parts of our nature. These parts are still there lurking in our unconscious though, and our dreams give us an opportunity to address and integrate these split off self-parts.

4. Level 4: Sod (Secret)

This is the deepest layer of the dream, often containing spiritual or mystical guidance. It is analogous to what Jung called "big" or highly important dreams. It can be the deepest layer found in many dreams, or conversely, it can be the whole dream in and of itself. When clearly understood, these dreams may have profound significance for our lives, and possibly the lives of those around us. Prophetic dreams belong in this category. We don't always find this layer; it is, after all, called *Sod*: secret. Years ago, my friend Janice worked on this dream type. She dreamt that she was wearing a white robe while presiding over some kind of ceremony, and saw herself lifting up her hands while standing in front of a crowd of people.

To work on this, we invited Jan to reenter her dream in her mind's eye while telling it, and then to experience the felt sense of herself wearing that robe. We asked her to actually lift her hands in the way she saw herself doing in the dream. As she physically reenacted this part of the dream, she connected it to her deep but unspoken desire to pursue a career in ministry. She had never actually articulated it before, but it clearly had not left her psyche.

A year later she made a decision and left the world of finance to enter divinity school. Looking at herself in the mirror three years later, she experienced a frisson of recognition: the ceremonial robe she was wearing for her ordination was practically identical to the one she had on in her dream four years earlier!

This deepest layer of the work can most often be accessed through dream reentry. This is done by purposefully reentering the landscape of the dream after you are awake, and traveling through it as a living journey, such as one may experience in a guided meditation. Your own dream is the landscape here, however, rather than a preset scene provided by someone else, like a beach or a forest. As well as providing personal messages, this layer may also provide us with a portal or passageway to other realms and alternate ways of knowing.

The final layer of dreamwork can be the transpersonal realm, the mystical layer—our connection with other times, other space, and the divine. It may be a remembering of ancient wisdom from our spiritual guides or ancestors. It can point us toward a path, a vision, or a hope as it did for Janice. Sometimes this layer shows up in the manifest content of the dream (that is, in the actual dream story as we dreamt it, the P'shat layer). When it comes to these dreams, we may just want to sit quietly with them and bask in the glow that is already present.

My client Terry dreamt that she was sitting in the lap of St. Teresa, her patron saint. This brought her a feeling of great comfort. All she needed or wanted to do with this dream, at least for the moment, was to enjoy the feeling of peace and blessing.

Examples of Working through Dreams
Using the PARDES Method

Here's a dream I had that I worked through using the PARDES method. To contextualize it, I had this dream a few months after my dad died. As you will see, I didn't realize it was connected to his death until working through the dream to the deeper layers.

I am in a grey snow and ice-locked landscape. I cross a small wooden bridge that has a guardian on it. He lets me by to enter a small but long wooden house that reminds me of a sauna. I then go out the other side of the house to a cold but bright sunny day. There is a river there that still has chunks of ice in it, but it is flowing freely and rushing past.

1. *P'shat (simple) layer:* This dream is set in winter. It is February here in real time as well, and dreary inside and outside the dream. I'd like to take a sauna to warm up because I hate being cold. I am glad that at least it is sunny outside at the end of the dream. The guardian captures my attention, and I wonder who or what he is.

2. *Remez (hinted at) layer:* I associate being cold with "having a cold," and catch the play on words here. I am congested and could use the warmth of a sauna to breathe better so that I am "flowing freely" again. I become aware of the emotions and physical sensations in my dream now; I feel both sad and numb with the cold. I have some initial associations to who that guardian may be: first to the guard at the gates of the Emerald City of Oz, and then to Cerbe-

rus, the three-headed dog that guards the gates of Hades in Greek mythology. Not yet sure which one I resonate with.

3. *Drash (pursued or revealed) layer:* I give this dream a title: "The Little Wooden House." I first associate that with the long houses of the Iroquois Nation, and then to the Little House series by Laura Ingalls Wilder. This is interesting but doesn't seem to get me any traction; it doesn't take me anywhere. It is a dead end. (Catch the pun.) So I next free associate to the guardian being a "guardian angel." This one resonates with me—I get an aha feeling. For the first time, I make the connection to my dad—that he is now one of my guardian angels. The title that I chose now takes me to the image of a coffin, which is also a "little wooden house." Death is cold. That guardian was the "guardian of the gates" between the worlds of life and death.

4. *Sod (secret) layer:* I realize that by the end of the dream, I have moved out of the landscape of being locked in ice, of being locked in my grief. I have gone out the other door and have begun moving on. It is still cold, but the bright sunny day gives me hope. Even though there are still chunks of ice in the water, it is now flowing, much like my own grief process. In waking life I am still sad, but returning to my routine activities more, since it has been about two months since he died. In the flowing of the water and the bright sunlight at the end of the dream, I feel a renewed connection with my dad. I now feel not sadness as I did initially, but comfort and even joy. He has become one of my guides, and I can contact him when I need advice. I now recognize the wooden bridge in the dream as the bridge between worlds that I can cross to be in contact with him. This is

the numinous layer of spiritual connection. It feels like all elements are accounted for now.

Finally, I'll share one more example of dreamwork that moves through these layers, but not sequentially. We can also weave back and forth between the various layers as information arises or is needed. This example demonstrates working on a dream in a therapy session. It includes references to various types of dreamwork methods that were used to help Josh move from one layer of the dream to the next. Further details on these methods will be covered in chapter 10 on revealing meanings in your dreams.

Josh dreamt that he entered a dark forest, following a man. The man then turned to him and Josh saw that he had a mask on. As he took it off, Josh realized that this man was not who he thought he was. The now unmasked man had a sinister smile on his face, and Josh felt lured in by him.

1. *P'shat:* Josh says, "In the dream I feel anxious about entering this forest, but feel compelled to do so. It seems kind of familiar to me, but can't quite place where it is. That man is creepy. I feel so stupid for having trusted him. Why is he masked; what is he hiding from me?"

2. *Remez:* When asked, the title Josh came up with was "Dangerous Seduction." He said, "It seems that this man wants to feed off me, but if I don't let him, he'll hurt me." I invite Josh to bring in allies and protection before going any further, by using the GAIA method (Guided Active Imagination Approach) to provide safety before working on a scary dream. We will examine this method in detail in chapter 11. As a Reiki practitioner, Josh brings in his guides and

"protection posse" in addition to surrounding himself with a bubble of white light. We tap into what might be the *Sod* or spiritual layer right here because of the need to set up safety before going further. I don't want Josh to be worrying about being hurt by the man in the dream as we explore it.

He now has an association to the man who wants to feed off him as a "vampire," and we talk about the concept of people who are "energy vampires" in his life. We play with what was needed to defend oneself against vampires, and come up with a cross and some garlic.

3. *Drash:* Now feeling safe enough to proceed—having as protection his guides, the white bubble of light, the cross, and the garlic—we use another active dreamwork technique and ask the dream character a question: "What do you want from me?" The man replies, "Validation and power." Interesting response. Josh is surprised by this answer (always a good sign in dreamwork).

Following this bit of active dreamwork, Josh gets a strong aha moment: "Oh, my. This man is my father and all of my ex-boyfriends—they all wanted something from me. They wanted to suck me dry and then leech off of me for their own gratification. I don't have to let them anymore. I have my spirituality (the cross) and my antibodies (garlic has antibiotic properties). I can protect myself now."

4. *Sod:* For the last bit of work, Josh and I make the connection that there is one more layer here—that of the shadow, the dark part of the self. Josh saw that in addition to representing others, this masked man was also a part of himself, the part of himself that ran away from or pushed others away. He said, "I think I must have masked this part

of myself in my dream because I wasn't proud of it. I feel embarrassed now even as I name it, but I know it is true." As we talked further, Josh realized that he developed this strategy to keep himself safe from those "energy vampires" in his life, but that it came at a cost as well.

Finally, he recognized the forest as a place he visited each summer in his childhood on family vacations, for better and for worse. That tied up the final loose end. (This last bit of information came through in this phase, even though it may fit more in the *Remez* or *Drash* layer; we take it when it comes.) Following the work on this dream, we now continue to do the psycho-spiritual healing and integration of this masked self-part that needs (as the masked dream man said) validation and a healthier type of power or empowerment. The title of Josh's dream changed from "Dangerous Seduction" to "Transformation." This change in the title highlights and mirrors the shift in the psyche as well.

EXERCISE

Examine one of your dreams using the PARDES system. It may be helpful to engage one or more others to help you sort through the layers, but you can certainly work through the dream on your own as well and see how far you get.

1. *P'shat*: First, simply write down your dream in as much detail as you can recall. Don't worry about how long or short it is; it can be a phrase or a longer storyline. It will be easier, however, to move through the four layers if you have a

somewhat longer dream to work with. Write down the details of the landscape or setting, as well as those of the characters and their actions.

2. *Remez:* Next, as you read over what you have written, see if any immediate associations occur to you. Notice your varied emotions and somatic responses about each part of the dream if you haven't already captured them. This emotional narrative is key in discerning what the dream is about. Does anything in the dream remind you of something in your waking life, either currently or in your past? Write down these associations next; don't censor or discard any of them yet. You'll decide later what is relevant to the dream. You may enjoy writing each layer in another color to help you keep track of what was in the original dream and what emerged as you followed the threads of connection.

3. *Drash:* Now, go over the dream and the associations you have captured and let your imagination go wild. Don't worry if what you come up with seems to have nothing to do with your original dream. You are following the threads here. Let yourself see if there are any puns or plays on words, connections to myth or fairy tales or movies. Look things up on Google to get more information about what they may mean outside of your dream, and see if anything registers as a hit or aha for you. Now try to connect the actual narrative of your dream with the new information that has

come through as you explore it to get a coherent sense of personal meaning. At this point, discard anything that was a false lead.

4. *Sod:* Finally, review your dream to see if there are any messages that may have meaning for others as well as yourself, or that contain any spiritual guidance, connection, or insight. Is there any part of the dream that could be prescriptive or prophetic? Is there any information you'd like to share with others as a result of having peeked through time? Remember that we do not always get to all the layers of a dream when we work on it. We may need to talk it through with others, and/or let it "warm up" over time, like that lemon, to get more juice from it. You can always come back to it again later.

Now that you've learned this system to help you navigate the layers of your dreams, let's turn to another aspect: the setting or the landscape itself. In this next layer of inquiry, we will examine landscape as a character in its own right, and discover what the locations of our dream adventures have to tell us about our lives and our journeys.

Six

FROM THE LANDSCAPE OF DREAMS TO LANDSCAPE OF THE SPIRIT

"A dream is a place; you don't have a dream,
you have an experience in a place."
Robert Moss

We are located *somewhere* in our dreams, in some setting or place, both as a psychic space and a landscape or environment where the dream takes place. Where we are in our dreams, as in life, is just as important as what happens there. This layer for understanding our dreams helps us to develop an appreciation not just for character and plotline, but also for the setting itself. Just as in any good story, the landscape or the setting of a dream can be an actual character, as well as the background that makes the foreground visible.

A sci-fi TV series called *Lost*, in which a plane crashed on an island and the survivors had multiple stranger-than-truth adventures, featured the setting of the Island as a living, breathing character in the story. The Island was sometimes intriguing, sometimes downright scary. Attention to place adds another layer to dreamwork as a vehicle for bringing us home. Our most important place is the one in which we feel at home. Laura Ingalls Wilder, author of the Little House series once said, "Home is the nicest word there is."

Sometimes we recognize the place in our dreams—we've been there before, or lived there, or seen it in a movie. Sometimes our dreamscape is nowhere that we recognize, but a curious or fantastic environment nonetheless. Sometimes the very stones speak to us, and sometimes the trees are dream characters. In Oz, for example, the apple trees are angry that their fruit is picked without permission, and they begin throwing apples when insulted. The setting is where we are in the dream, and we have to start with where we are to be able to orient ourselves to where we are going.

Recurring Places

Recurring dreams or dream themes indicate to us that something is important. Sometimes they keep on coming simply to underline their importance, but sometimes they will return in one form or another until we "get" the message they are trying to convey to us, then do something about it. Dreaming of the same place or a similar landscape can have the same function. We are meant to pay attention and learn something. The dream landscape is a portal into a time and place that has meaning for us.

For example, if we frequently have dreams that are set in our childhood home, it is likely that there is something about that time in our life that is relevant for us today—perhaps in the category of "unfinished business"—or some connection wants to be made between our present and our past. To orient to the place, you can ask questions of yourself and your dreams, such as:

- When you lived in that childhood home with the blue house and the black shutters, how old were you? And how old are you in the dream?

- What was happening at that time in your life?

- What about that time in your life is relevant in your life today?

Here's an example:

> Kevin kept having vaguely anxious recurring dreams about the house he lived in when he was six years old. In working back and forth between the dream and life, he realized that he had lived in that house during a time of great turmoil when his parents were divorcing and he didn't know who would be living where when the dust settled. He felt very out of control back then, and remembered walking around his house taking mental snapshots of the rooms and the furniture and where his toys and books were in case he wouldn't be able to live there anymore. He showed me what he did by holding up his hands in front of his face and saying "click" as he pushed one finger down on the "button" of the camera.

Neither parent wanted to give up the home, and it became a source of contention in the divorce. When I asked if he was currently feeling any of this sense of displacement or insecurity in his life, he replied that the company he worked for was being sold, and he had no idea if he would have a job when the transaction was complete. Connecting these two disparate times in his life, Kevin could then recognize that he was experiencing many of the same feelings of being uprooted, out of control, and insecure about his future that he had when he was six years old. Once this dream-to-life landscape connection was identified, he began to identify not only the similarities but also the differences between the life changes he had no control over at age six and the ones occurring in the present.

Now, as an adult with good skills, a solid work history, and a severance package if needed, he had the ability to take action and make choices in his life that he didn't have as a six-year-old. Recognizing the fact that, as an adult, Kevin had more control in his life than he did as a child going through the trauma of family separation was key. Once he made the connection, he stopped having the repetitive anxious dreams featuring his childhood home, and instead could begin to feel some excitement about new possibilities.

When we experience some kind of disconnection in our lives, our dreams may guide us to recognize our yearning and longing to be home. Feeling stuck, blocked, isolated, sick, or in the throes of a major life transition, like Kevin, can alert us to the need to be able to carry our home inside of our own being. Our soft animal selves want to feel the security of shelter. When we follow the ideas our dreams have shown us and take steps to find or re-find ourselves, we can also find ourselves back home.

Nothing feels more like home than speaking or hearing the language you grew up with. For the person who grew up speaking a different language than the one they speak currently, speaking or hearing their mother tongue in a dream can instantly transport them to times and places in their distant past. Like the childhood home in Kevin's dream, a native language can point toward a formative time of life or event. Dreams can be oblique and indirect in their references, simply pointing in a direction and leaving it up to us to explore and explain that terrain.

My friend Marcia had a dream of a snake-like being called a "Ruah." Not coming up with any associations with that word that made any sense, we began looking it up to see if it meant something in another language. The closest we came was to the word *ruach*, which means spirit or wind in Hebrew. Once this connection to her spiritual language was made, Marcia was able to start making connections to the regenerative aspects of this snake who could shed its skin as it grew and the regenerative quality of spirit the word represented for her, and how it applied to her current life transitions.

For those of you who grew up speaking more than one language, or have learned other languages as an adult, it is curious and interesting to notice which language you dream in. Does it change from dream to dream? From topic to topic? What do you associate with dreaming in one language or another? If you dream in your mother tongue, the language of your first home, does it stand to reason that the dream has something to do with your childhood, even if that is not part of the manifested content of your dream? This is an interesting avenue to explore.

A recurring "dreamscape" can be like any recurring symbol, pointing to the importance of this place in our lives. It can also be an internal dream code indicating, "Heads up, this is a dream." For several years my unconscious decided to announce, "Hello, different reality here!" by setting my dreams in the country that I had previously inhabited. During the course of nearly two decades, the majority of my dreams began, "I am in Israel and…" then a story would unfold. I lived in Israel during my twenties, so I recognized the dream landscape and the time of life it referred to, but the deeper meanings eluded me. With a little help from my friends I was finally able to suss out the meaning. I recognized that one layer of meaning for this landscape was code for "alternate reality." In one dream I am in the desert dancing in a line of robed and veiled Bedouin women toward a large tent, where powerful drumming is calling us in. In another dream I am standing on a sea of sand, seeing the shimmering heat waves rise up. In another more daily-life type theme, I dream that I am promoted to a new job in Israel.

I actually began my professional career there, going to graduate school and working with teenage girls in a development town. The land itself was both foreground and background to my life during those years, and I hiked on it a lot during my free time. Even though the "code for dreamtime" interpretation of why my dreams were so often set in Israel made sense, I could feel that there was more to be learned. Another layer was waiting to be recognized. I continued to search for that additional layer of meaning to these recurring landscapes, and next discovered shamanic implications.

Dreams and Shamanic Practice

Shamanic practice teaches that we can inadvertently leave a part of ourselves behind in a place. If we do so, we have to go back to retrieve that part in order to be fully whole again. In his book *Meditation*, Songa Rinpoche, a renowned meditation teacher, tells us, "Meditation is bringing the lost parts home." Meditation, shamanic practice, and dreamwork have much in common. These recurring places may appear to us in our dreams to let us know that we have to make the journey back, either literally or figuratively or both, to complete some part of our personal mythic journey and reclaim the wholeness of our being.

We can feel a sense of yearning or longing for something perhaps unnamed, maybe located as a sensation around the heart that we feel from time to time. It might be felt as a passion or a curiosity, as homesickness or a bittersweet tug associated with some place, setting, or landscape in your life or your dream. It may be that a part of you has been left there, needing to be retrieved and brought back home. Like Kevin's dreams about his childhood home, or my dreams about being in Israel, recurring dreams can point us toward a time when something essential about ourselves got lost, stuck, or forgotten.

Once I discovered this shamanic teaching of the reclamation of parts of oneself, I began to wonder what I had left there, and the dreams began to transform. I gave attention to their message and to figuring out how to take action in response. This is a key part of active and embodied dreamwork—to not only understand what your dreams are telling you, but to integrate their teachings and then to go out into the world and actually do some action because of it. Robert Moss called this piece of dreamwork "the

Bridge to Life." The key to truly transformative dreamwork is to go out and do something based on the message from your dream.

When I decoded this deeper meaning of my Israel dreams, my next step in response to these dream teachings was to find friends near Boston, where I lived, and with whom I could speak Hebrew again. I studied for and had an adult bat mitzvah, found a teacher, Reb Gershon Winkler, to study Jewish shamanism with, and then celebrated my daughter's bat mitzvah when she turned twelve. These actions began to fill in a part of myself that I hadn't even realized had been missing since I left that landscape, that country that later became the portal to my dreams. Finally, I visited Israel after a twenty-five year absence and reconnected with old friends and familiar places. That seemed to be the final step. I reclaimed the physicality of this missing piece of myself by literally going back to find it.

Nowadays, the landscapes of my dreams are much more rich and varied. By understanding the message of my recurring dream landscapes and taking a variety of actions to resolve the under-lying dynamics, I reclaimed the part of myself that had been left behind. In the process, I freed up space in my dream life for new vistas and horizons to come through.

When we recognize the spirit of place in dreams, we renew our place of spirit. As we live in the sacredness of our dream landscapes and establish a relationship with the lands of our dreams, we open up a portal to living in sacredness in our waking world as well.

Creating Sacred Place in Our Waking Dreamscape

From the perspective of the waking dream, that liminal space of intuition and synchronicities, there are dreams of place, and places of dreams. We know that we can dream while asleep and also have waking dreams that are equivalent to the deeper meaning of our nighttime dreams. As we pay attention to our surroundings and to the synchronicities that may appear for us, we can all dream while awake. Druids know that the living spirits of the woods and of nature inhabit the trees themselves in the forms of nymphs and dryads and other "tree people."

In his book *Dream Tending*, psychologist Stephen Aizenstat speaks of the concept of an "ensouled world." He writes, "In order to live rich meaningful lives, we must live as if the world around us is alive, has a soul, and is filled with meaning in every nook and cranny, its every animal, rock and tree."

This concept of an ensouled world is key to the integration of our bodies, minds, and personal souls with the great All-Soul of the world, and with our ability to be at home in the greater world and in our own skins. When we see all as holy, then we too are holy. We can then find that spark of the divine more easily within ourselves, within our dreams, and in the world around us. A number of Native American tribes descending from the Anishinabek referred to America as "Turtle Island." They lived daily life in recognition of the waking dream of the sacredness of the land and of all beings. Thus the whole continent was home for them, as it was for the turtle within her shell.

Native Americans, Druids, and our mystic poets like Blake and Emerson all refer to the "in-between" places we can stumble into or seek out in the world, where ordinary and nonordinary reality intersect, where the profane and the sacred meet, and where the place of holiness is found within our perception. It is there all along, but we need the eyes of our hearts to see it. Shamanic artist Carol Dearborn hints at this when she says in her blog at caroldearborn.com, "It appears that there is a 'place' … in the intersection of the perceptual/cognitive process (a 'place' or type of brainwave), between waking and sleep where the meta-physical intersects the physical. This intersection … becomes a kind of portal through which energy can be conveyed … Opening this portal requires a receptive and reverential state of being, like falling in love." This too is a sacred place. Jung called these spaces just between waking and sleeping the hypnopompic and hypnagogic zones. We can have sacred space in our dream worlds, in our waking worlds, and in the spaces and places in between.

Place is such an important aspect of holiness that one of the words for God in Hebrew is *makom*, meaning "place." The word contains both a temporal implication (time-based) as well as a physical one. The presence of holiness can become so infused in a place that the place itself becomes synonymous with holiness. Perhaps the most common example of place becoming holy because of what occurs there is Mount Sinai, the place where Moses received the Ten Commandments. The same word, *makom,* also appears in Genesis in the creation story (the Garden of Eden is the first sacred place), and when Moses encounters the burning bush (at a particular place, *makom,* in the desert). When we are at *makom* we are for a moment outside of the ordinary rules of time and space, and for that moment on holy ground. Sacred place may thus be defined as a place that hosts an encounter with the divine.

Joyce's Dream

Here is an example of this intersection between waking life and waking dream experienced by my friend Joyce, who defines her waking dream as, "Paying attention to something extraordinary happening in everyday life as a strong internal message." Her narration begins with something that happened to her in waking life.

She told us that she was in the Pyrenees in northern Spain on a hiking trip. She brought her old comfortable hiking boots from REI, so no worries about blisters or foot pain. After hiking for about two hours on this very hot day, they stopped for a break at a twelfth-century hermitage. It is a sacred site and oasis where individuals worshipping God in medieval times might have come on a pilgrimage. As they left to continue their hike, the soles of her shoes suddenly began to peel off, first the right shoe and then the left. There was now nothing left between the bottom of her feet and the rocks. With several hours of hiking left to do and no possibility of a vehicle coming to the rescue, she had a problem. Her hiking guide, Marco, then remembered that he had sandals in his backpack. He put them on and gave her his orange sneakers, which fit. They continued on the hike. Later that day, Marco took her to buy new hiking shoes.

As Joyce reflects on this event, she realizes the deeper significance of it. In mythos, arriving at a sacred place is often a beginning of a transformation or a change in a journey. In this sacred hermitage in the mountains, she lost her "old soles/souls." They no longer served her on her journey. Not just one sole, but both, as though placing an exclamation mark in this message. Something ended. She couldn't go on in the middle of nowhere with just her socks on a very rocky path. An energetic "door" opened and her guide (Marco) pulled out handmade sandals with long leather straps from his backpack. They looked like something an ancient biblical ancestor would wear in the desert. He put them on and tied them high over his ankles. Then he gave her his bright orange sneakers, which fit perfectly. She followed him out of the valley for the rest of the day, wondering where else he was leading her, besides to their rest stop for the evening.

Later on, Marco (the Guide, now capitalized because he's guiding her in a deeper sense, whether he knows it or not) takes her to buy new "souls" at a store. Joyce choose the only pair that fit, which happened to be the exact brand and style of a pair she had at home which were tattered and ready to be given away. She got the insight that the shoes she bought are at once "new soles" and "knew souls" (souls of persons that she has known in this life or another.)

Joyce goes on to wonder what it meant to lose her "soles," put on the "souls" of her Guide, and follow in his footsteps. She wonders what she was shedding, or what is being asked of her in terms of "grounding," since she suddenly couldn't walk on the earth. Marco is on one level just a guy leading a hiking trip, but at the same time also a spiritual guide taking her from the old to the new. She feels that she is being led somewhere and a new phase is unfolding.

Joyce is describing for us the numinous experience of her intersecting worlds of sacred and ordinary time. She experiences the magic in the mundane, while to another it might have simply been a lucky coincidence that someone else's shoes fit when hers fell apart. Her own perception and interpretation allowed her to see with new eyes and find a deeper meaning in these events.

You may want to try this yourself: Notice some unusual or out of the ordinary events in your life, and breathe into them an expansive awareness that makes room for messages and magic. Take yourself to the threshold, suspend disbelief, and see what emerges.

Ritual and Place

In addition to being open to the possibility of a waking dream encounter as Joyce was on her hiking journey through the Pyrenees, ritual can often aid us in bringing down this place of eyes-wide wonder and creating sacred space in seemingly random locations. Ritual helps to convey the spiritual dimension of an activity. Joyce discovered her waking dream by reviewing her real-life experience through the lens of dreamtime.

Next is an example of creating a waking dream encounter using ritual to cross the veil between worlds and connect with our loved ones who have passed over. I was walking in the woods with my friend Sara about a month after her grandfather had died. Earlier that day she had declined her rabbi's offer to say kaddish, the prayer for the dead, since it is usually said only for parents, spouses, or children.

When I asked her if she regretted that, without hesitation she said, "Yes, and I rarely regret anything!" We walked a little more, and then I wondered out loud, "Would you like to say kaddish now?" She agreed, with alacrity. Since she had already received permission from her rabbi to expand the circle of people one would usually say kaddish for, we agreed that it would also be okay to be creative with the requirement of needing a minimum of ten people, called a minyan, for this particular prayer. Tuning in to Aizenstat's concept of the ensoulment of all beings, Sara said "Yes, let's find a nice tree we can stand near to say it."

So we bushwhacked through some weeds to get really close to a beautiful three-trunked tree, one of those "triple goddess trees." Sara decided that ten nature beings, including us, would do just fine. She said, "She (the Tree) could be part of our minyan of ten, along with Bodhisattva" (her dog, who was with us—and yes, that was her actual doggy name). We got into the spirit of minyan (ten), and began counting: "Me, you, Bodi. That's three. The triple tree counts as three, that's six. Then the earth, the sky, that low bush, and the rish-roosh sound of the wind spirit in the trees. That's ten." We had our minyan. Ten beings. We said kaddish.

The dreaming spirits of the place came through, and we crossed the threshold into an extraordinary reality in the woods. We could sense the spirit of her grandfather join us, and had a lovely gathering in this in-between place. Perhaps the Druidic spirits of the trees also joined us in the minyan. As E. E. Cummings wrote in his *Complete Poems, 1904-1962*, "thank you God for this most amazing day, for the leaping greenly Spirit of the trees."

EXERCISE

To bring your attention to the element of place in your dreams, start by fleshing out the landscape you have dreamed about. Write it out in great detail: notice the topography, the climate, the season, and the flora and fauna that may be there. Then check to see if this is a place you have actually visited or lived in, or whether it is a dreamscape from your mind's eye. What does it feel like to be there? Notice the emotions that accompany this place and time. If you have dreams with reoccurring places, pay special attention. What happened in that place in your life? Is there a part of you left behind there that needs to be reclaimed?

In addition, you can create sacred space through the intentionality you bring to the place you are in. Do you need a ritual in a particular space to consecrate it? Looking with soft eyes, with both your inner and your outer vision, can also help you to see the dream world in waking life and gain the wisdom and the gifts hidden in plain sight wherever you find yourself.

Seven

·······························

IMAGERY: THE LIVING
CORE OF THE DREAM

"Every night for a hundred years the angel of
dreams came to the town and splashed the
walls with bright colors that stayed until the
first light of day."
Brian Andreas

At the core of our dreams are images. Beautiful, frightening, sensual, intriguing—they usually represent the heart of our dreaming landscapes. Psychiatrist Ernest Hartman coined the phrase the "Central Image" (or CI) to help us quickly zero in on that core message in our dreams. To find your CI, look for the image that contains the most pop and the most sizzle amidst the clutter of the details—that will be the core of your dream. If you don't know where to start when working on a dream, start there. Let yourself get to know this image well; it will invariably lead you home to the key message that the dream has come to give you.

Finding the central image is one shortcut for cutting to the chase in dreamwork. It is the image or symbol or action that stands out in some way with particular vividness or clarity or bizarreness. If we put our attention on the dream as a whole, what jumps out at us? It may not be what we expect. If we are surprised by our response, all the better—that means we have set aside our preconceived notions of what we thought we knew and have allowed our unconscious wisdom to guide us. This is part of the joy in doing dreamwork, the delight of the surprise.

For example, workshop member Jennifer dreamed that she was walking on the beach. There were a number of other people around. One woman was wearing a bright red dress over her blue bathing suit. There were children shouting and playing with a large multicolored beach ball. She felt herself getting hot and thinking about going into the water to swim when she woke. This dream has a number of details, but when I asked her to focus on a central image, the red dress stood out. So that is where we started, exploring the meaning of a dress, the color red, and associations to this particular dress in her dream.

The CI contains the emotional core of the dream. As we work with a dream, we need to name and differentiate between the varied emotions it contains in order to know the personal meaning of the images for ourselves. If we feel shaded or refreshed by that eucalyptus tree or feel sexy in that red dress in our dream, that is a different emotional response than if we feel strangled by the tree or too exposed or uncomfortable in that dress. The differing emotional responses we have to the images indicate the core meaning of those images for us, and point us toward different actions in our lives that may be needed in response to the dream.

Lately I've been paying more attention to the living nature of these dream images. In *Dream Tending,* Aizenstat opens up the concept of imagery to include what he calls the "living image." Drawing on the work of Carl Jung and other Jungian dream-workers such as James Hillman and Marion Woodman, Aizenstat shares his view that dream images are not static. He tells us that the images in our dreams have a life of their own, and that they exist in the outside world as well as in the one we have dreamed them in. Our relationship with the images may start inside our dreams, but as we animate them in our dreamwork they come alive for us in our waking world as well.

As we make note of the images that have been brought forward to our conscious mind by the dream, we may also start to see them appear more and more in our daily life. Once we have been made aware of something, it enters our consciousness, and if we are paying attention we begin to notice it more. We see more of what we are looking for. This is a neurological as well as psychological and mystical phenomenon. The question may not be how often do we see a hummingbird, but how often do we notice that we are seeing a hummingbird. This mindful awareness connects our central dream images with the synchronicities and meaningful coincidences of daily life to create a seamless weave between our sleeping worlds and our waking worlds, thus bringing us toward greater unity of our soul and soul purpose.

Pattern Recognition and How the Image Exists Outside of the Dream

In his book *Field, Form, and Fate*, Michael Conforti approaches the same concept as Aizenstadt but from the opposite direction. He speaks of the *a priori,* or pre-existing nature of the image. This image represented in our dream already exists in the world of matter and physical life. Therefore, Conforti teaches that in order to really understand what the image is trying to tell us inside our dream, we have to move outside of the dream to understand how it actually exists in the waking world. Learning physical details about the image that appears in our dream assists us in understanding the deepest layers of what is has come to tell us. So, how does this work?

For example, let's say you dreamt of a tree. Now find out exactly what kind of tree it is, and then do some research about it. If you dreamt of a eucalyptus tree, you need to explore the natural habitat of a eucalyptus tree, how big it tends to get, how much water it needs, what it is used for, and where you might find one. In your dream, did this tree grow in correspondence with its natural and usual habitat, or was it found in a different and unusual place? Have you ever had a personal encounter with a tree like this in your life, and if so, when?

Using our scryer Google, I discovered that eucalyptus trees are in the myrtle family, are indigenous to Australia, are very fast growing, have medicinal qualities, are water guzzlers and often planted to drain swamps and reduce the risk of malaria, can be used as a natural insecticide, and are frost-intolerant. So if this particular tree showed up in our dream, as opposed to a weeping willow or a maple, how does the a priori nature of a eucalyptus tree inform our dream and our life? This image can now provide us with information about somewhere in our life we may need to drain something off (dare I say, drain a swamp), or where we need to protect ourselves from frost or frosty people in our life, or where we need to be protected from being "bugged" (hitting the insecticide association), or where we need to find a way to quickly get some new growth going.

The meaning of the symbol is thus embedded in the actual form of the thing itself. So, it is still a tree, with all of the associations we might have to trees in general (growth, green, strength, family trees or roots, mystical connotations, tree of life, etc.), but it is also a specific tree that carries specific associations. I did not know most of these qualities of the eucalyptus tree before I Googled it (except for the draining the swamp one, I knew about that), and would have missed most of these image-specific messages had I not looked further.

When we get to know our personal dream images and patterns, we can then make the connections between the images, the features of the waking world, and the patterns of our lives as a whole. Knowledge is power, so with this greater knowledge of our inner worlds, we can make choices about the life patterns we want to continue and those we want to change. Without this knowledge, we are led around by the leash of unconscious repetition of our old patterns—and often by the leashes of the inherited patterns from the lives of our parents and grandparents as well. This is the essence of what are sometimes called "legacy burdens."

Conforti reminds us that pattern recognition is essential for survival: animals in the wild need to recognize the pattern of the seasons and the natural order of things in order to be able to squirrel away enough food for the coming winter or escape from danger by reading the signs that alert them to its approach. The animals know—they are already running to higher ground way before the humans are aware that the tsunami is approaching. We too can learn to read subtle signals and patterns important for our survival, which can tell us things like who in our lives is trustworthy and who is not, or when and how to trust our intuition about something, even if our left brain has not caught up to the message yet. (This was one of the messages that Sue, our fox dreamer, was working on: who and when to trust.) And even if we can't yet change some of the dynamics of our lives, we can change our response to them, which in and of itself can be life-changing.

Our dreams can help us to find and then make these choices. In the spirit of being able to make life choices and control our responses to matters outside of our control, noted psychiatrist and Holocaust survivor Viktor Frankl, in *Man's Search for Meaning*, writes, "The last of the human freedoms [is] to choose one's attitude in any given set of circumstances, to choose one's own way." That is where we still have complete freedom, a gift of the dream.

Our images are real to us as we dream them. Vividly alive in our night journeys, the images can enrich our lives and bring us closer and closer to our soul's home if we allow them to become animated in our daytime world by actively engaging with them there. Aizenstadt's basic premise is that dreams are alive. If we accept that premise, then the images can be interacted with any time, day or night.

Take a moment to think about your most vividly remembered dream images. Some are more real than the book you are holding right now, or the chair or bed you are sitting on. Can't you practically taste them? ("Tasting a dream" is a type of synesthesia, which is both a cross-wiring of the senses and the experience of them in an alternate sense, a common dream phenomenon.)

EXERCISE

To get a taste of the vividness and aliveness of a sensory experience, try seeing or feeling the following dream image. After you read the words, close your eyes for a moment to capture it.

You are sitting at your campfire in the night-dark woods, the last one of your friends awake, smelling the wood smoke, feeling drowsy, with the lingering taste of chocolatey marshmallow s'mores in your mouth. You startle and sit up as yellow eyes with thin black slits of pupils pop out of the darkness just a few feet in front of you. Just eyes—yellow eyes—staring straight at you.

Can you feel the hair on the back of your neck stand up as you imagine those eyes?

Our Personal Dream Mythos

When we interact with the images from our dreams and give them attention outside of the dream, we engage in a process Jung called *amplification*, or making something larger. When we expand the image past our own personal story we enter the realm of myth and archetype—the grand stories that have engaged humankind for millennia. We dream nightly in our own personal mythologies. Our waking task is to connect our dreams with larger-world mythologies and see ourselves in the greater context of being part and parcel of the human condition.

Here is an example of connecting our dreams into a larger context, found in two dreams with mythic undertones and a powerful CI. Jana, a member of my dream group, shared them with us. She first dreamed that she was living in a tent with other Israelites in the desert. There were holes in the tent and hail fell through on her and the others in the tent. It reminded her of the plagues in Egypt.

Her second dream, about three days later, continued one of the themes in a different way. She dreamed that she was in bed in her tent at summer camp. Two girls were whispering outside her tent window, and she told them that they woke her up. One girl replied, "You're never confined to the tent that you're in."

Those back to back dreams also exemplify the importance of writing dreams down, since we may have missed the repeating theme otherwise. The repetition of the tent imagery from the first dream in the second alerts us to the fact that it's a central image and provides the dream circle with avenues to follow while unpacking and examining Jana's tent dreams.

Jana's first dream connects her personal image of the tent with a psycho-spiritual journey that is common mythos in Western culture. It references the journey of the Israelites out of slavery in Egypt and through the desert of Sinai on their way to the Promised Land in the book of Exodus. This motif is not just Judeo-Christian, but one common to African-Americans as a metaphor for their own ongoing journey from slavery to freedom—a frequent and powerful theme in gospel music. Every year on Passover we read of the ten plagues that were inflicted on the Pharaoh and his people before he finally allowed the Israelites to leave Egypt. One of the plagues is hail, just as in Jana's dream. Jana's first dream immediately connects her with these larger stories, and the recurring image of the tent lets us know that the second dream is somehow connected as well.

Using *a priori* meaning to guide your thought process, look at the striking connective image in the two dreams and ask yourself, "What is a tent?" We got a variety of responses from the dream circle, many of them related to the idea of home. Members tapped into their own associations that a tent is a form of shelter— usually a temporary shelter in our day and age, but a permanent one in ancient times. Tents as shelter and as home are ubiquitous for many indigenous and native people. It was and still is a portable home that can be carried on the back while journeying. It is a way to protect against the elements when we are exposed. Many of these associations resonated with our dreamer.

Both the desert tent with holes that let in the hail in the first dream, and the intrusion into her sleep in the second dream reminded Jana of the lack of protection she was feeling in several areas of her home life. She told us about feeling "enslaved" by a number of physical illnesses she suffered over the years, some acute and some chronic. A writer and artist, she described to us how she used to wake up in the mornings bursting with ideas and imagery, how she couldn't wait to see the kids off to school so she could get to work. But the last few years had felt like a dry desert—her own personal wilderness. Her first dream tent appeared in the Sinai desert and had holes in it, leaving Jana unprotected from the hail. In the second dream, she was advised that she had the option of changing tents. We needed to find out what this meant to her.

As we worked more with these images, Jana analyzed her life for areas where she felt unprotected, dried up, or pelted by something hard and cold. Could she repair the holes in the tent of the first dream, or the metaphorical holes in parts of her home life where she felt unprotected? Or was it in fact time to consider a different tent? The second dream tent enlarged the image of the first one, telling her quite clearly that she was not required to stay in that tent.

We encouraged her to see what it felt like over the next few weeks to live in these tents, to journal on it, to imagine herself there, to feel in her bones and skin what could be repaired or changed to feel more "at home" and more protected. Knowing that she was not confined to the tent she was in gave her the freedom to imagine many possible options for her marriage and home life.

Images from our dreams can connect us in a positive or a negative way to our sense of home. Some of our dream images live with us long after the rest of the dream itself has faded. Are you carrying around in your mind's eye the remaining image of a whorled shell, or the sound of a cat purring, or the smell and sensation of rough, wet wool against your skin as you walk in the rain in your wool cloak? Your dreams might contain obvious home images of a house, a tent, a lean-to, an igloo, or a cave. Can you make any connections between your own dreams and mythos, fairy tales, or religious works? Take note of these powerful images and how they relate to your life.

Next let's examine methods for working with these images.

Working with the Image to Gain Meaning: Association, Amplification, Animation, and Embodiment

Jung provides three steps for the process of enlivening your dream images: association, amplification, and animation.

First, freely *associate* with the image. Allow your mind to spontaneously wander about and connect to whatever comes up for you from your own life, feelings, and memories, whether or not you understand the connection right away.

Then you *amplify*, or enlarge these associations to find the bigger stories. These new directions may not even be part of the original dream, but the dream helps to point you in this direction.

Finally, you *animate*, bringing the image to life. One way to animate a dream image is to embody it, to feel, sense, and move it in your body.

I'll illustrate this process by showing how I worked with one of my dream images: a large, bright blue-green bird with a very long tail flew into my room. It was beautiful but a little scary, since it was fluttering around the room and was so big. I wondered if I should let it out or try to catch it first. Then I realized that it was a quetzal.

My first waking associations were with my father-in-law's tame parrot, then to the mythical phoenix, and then to my cats' personal "catch and release" program. When a bird accidentally gets into our house they catch but don't kill it. I then capture and release. I didn't really know what a quetzal was when I had the dream, only that it had to do with Central America. I amplified the image to find out more, and sought out the advice of my dream circle.

To find the *a priori* meaning of the word, we searched the internet for quetzal and found references to a divine bird associated with the Mayan and Aztec religions in Mexico. It is officially called a "resplendent quetzal," and is associated with divinity, love, and air; its plumage was once highly valued for use in the headdresses of royalty. Wow! I loved that it is called "resplendent." My body began to fill up with the airborne feeling of the quetzal and I spontaneously began to embody it by spreading my arms wide and waving them at shoulder level. Now I could feel this quetzal energy in my body, especially around my heart and the place behind my heart on my back where my wings would be. After that, using a technique of dream re-entry (which we will cover in detail in chapter 10), I went back into the dream and I decided to leave the window to my room open so that the quetzal could come and go freely.

By using this method of association (seeing what about the dream image caught at my attention), then amplifying (enlarging the story, broadening it to include worldwide mythic associations), and then embodying and animating the image, my interaction with the dream image came to life. I felt exhilarated, a little frightened, and a bit awed by the size and beauty of this splendid bird. Notice that I didn't come away from the work on it knowing exactly what it "meant" to dream this dream. Instead, the work took me into an embodied process, rather than a more linear "this means that" form of dreamwork, encouraging me to leave the window in my soul open for this energy and beauty to come through. I didn't need to get more specific than that for the moment. The embodied reenacting of the wingspan of the quetzal gave me a felt sense of the message beyond words.

There is always something we can do to embody and honor the image in a dream, to add a layer of meaning and insight to the dreamwork. If we can't act it out we might still light a candle or plant a tulip bulb—any simple physical act that makes a place in waking time for our dream images to live. Our unconscious mind will resonate with this action and ultimately reward us with a deepening of our understanding of the dream and its meaning for our life when the image and our life are ripe for it.

Dream images are poetry of the soul.

Here in New England we celebrate spring after a long harsh winter. Themes of renewal, resurrection, and freedom abound as we punctuate this season with Easter, Passover, and the equinox. Often, snow still blankets the ground as the green shoots and buds push through the earth, reminding us that what has been buried underground all winter has not died. It's just been waiting to have enough light and warmth to erupt forth with new life. Found within the images of even our darkest dreams and night-mares are the roots of our growth and renewal. As we struggle to rise up through the layers of sleep to our dream-saturated waking consciousness, retaining what we can of the messages that came through to us in the night, we can find the hints of our healing.

Poet Mary Oliver slays me with her words. The following excerpt, which comes from her book *Dream Work,* is titled "Dreams." It's full of rich, luscious, gorgeous images. Here she describes vividly the felt sense of the nightly dreams we drag with us into the morning light of conscious awareness:

All night
the dark buds of dreams
open
richly...
... and you drag from the ground
the muddy skirt of your roots
and leap awake
with two or three syllables
like water in your mouth
and a sense
of loss—a memory
not yet of a word,
certainly not yet the answer—
only how it feels
when deep in the tree
all the locks click open,
and the fire surges through the wood,
and the blossoms blossom.

Oliver uses the richly evoked images in her poem to capture that feeling of "almost-ness" we have when we wake with a felt sense of the dream, but often with nothing more than an image or two remaining. We "almost" get the message. Then, when we grasp the meaning of our core image, we can feel those "locks click open" with the "*oh*" or "*aha*" of a newly minted truth resonating in our body and mind.

Have you ever had a dream that was so vivid, so sensual that you could practically smell or taste it? That's what my colleague Laurie's dream of honey was like, a dream we will explore next, one filled with drippy sweetness, full for the senses. And the fact that she is a consummate storyteller, and acted it out spontaneously while telling it, made it that much more delicious. She stopped me in the hallway on campus to tell me this dream. She reported that in the dream she was rushing around doing very busy things, teaching her class, preparing notes. Then across the way was a very large, clear glass jar, like the kind used at banquets, containing slices of orange or lemon and water filled with honey. The spigot seemed to be open, so it was dripping thick golden honey. She said that she didn't see a container, so she rushed over and put her hand under the jar to catch the honey. And she said, "Rushing back to my busyness over here, rushing to catch honey over there. Rushing back again to busyness over here, then rushing back again to catch the sweet sticky honey in my hands over there." Finally she stopped and just caught the honey. Laurie acted it out while telling it, demonstrating the rushing about here and there, and how she had her hands under the spigot.

Listening to her dream, I was so engaged that I could barely restrain myself from interrupting to make comments or ask questions. (The reason for practicing restraint at this juncture is that it is important to just listen to the dream before responding. We want to respect the dreamer and her dream by not getting in the way until they are ready for feedback, as well as simply not intruding on their experience.) Luckily, Laurie was both entertaining enough and insightful enough that I managed to wait until she finished, then said something simple, such as, "How wonderful—you were catching sweetness with both hands." In that way I simply followed her into her dream while avoiding the temptation to put my stamp on it.

Laurie told me that the messages she had already received from the dream were about the importance of slowing down her busyness, even stopping what she was doing, in order to catch the sweetness of life. Also, she considers part of her job to catch and appreciate the sweetness that her students bring to her class. Who wouldn't want a teacher like that!

Because we were in a public place when she told me the dream, we didn't work on any of its other layers. (Warning: If you become known as a dreamworker, you too may have friends and acquaintances stopping you in random places to tell you their dreams.) But I was left with my own strong image of the honey, and began my own internal process of exploring "If this were my dream …" As I expanded into, or embodied, the living image of the honey, I could feel and taste the sweetness on my tongue, more raw and gritty than sugar. I thought about bees, and beehives, and honeycomb, and the queen bee with her worker bees.

My associations next took me to how I don't like the feeling of stickiness on my hands. Then I segued to an old folksong about cooking with honey. I next remembered that honey also has antibiotic properties, and was used in wound healing before the advent of antibiotics. After that I caught the phrase "sweet dreams." Finally I recalled that I recently got a message on Facebook about a wonderful morning health drink of hot water with lemon, organic honey, and cinnamon, which I started drinking.

My sweet digression generated two takeaways. One, you can get as much mileage out of someone else's dream as your own, as I resonated to my own images and remembrances of honey that had nothing to do with Laurie's dream. And two, there is always some hidden core of healing that we can get to if we keep working at it, which were my associations to the antibiotic properties of honey and the healthy honeyed drink.

In the next chapter, we move our inquiry from the meanings of the images to working with them to enhance our creativity and our healing.

EXERCISE

Find the central image from a recent dream to work with. I recommend trying to use your body, not your brain, to find this central image. Try to quiet your mind and just let the image that most wants your attention to emerge. If you are surprised by what jumps out at you, even better. That means that you have successfully bypassed your conscious mind and allowed the wisdom of your unconscious to take center stage. If more than one emerges, choose the one that stands out for you in its vividness and uniqueness. Then allow yourself to free associate to it, not rejecting any ideas at this juncture, just like brainstorming. If you write them down, you will have a compendium of associations to refer back to. When you've reached the end of your own associations, ask others for their connections to your image, and/or Google it to get a wide variety of meanings. Sit with all these ideas and let them percolate. See which ones have meaning for you.

You can also make a pictorial outline to see all the associations at once. Draw a circle on paper with spokes radiating out from it, like a child's drawing of the sun. Write the image from your dream in the center of the circle, and then put all of your own and others' associations at the ends of the spokes. Some people like to use one color for their own associations and another color for those that came from others. As you look at the picture, circle the ones that resonate as meaningful to your dream. We will look at how to use art to enhance and illustrate your dreams more explicitly in the next chapter.

You can also work with Jung's three ways of living into the dream, finding out for yourself what happens when you amplify (make larger than life, connect to larger stories and mythos) and embody (feel into and/or move as well as associate to the images). Notice if there are repeating themes and patterns. These will have extra resonance and importance for you. Look up the *a priori* meaning that exists outside of your dreams, and see how they may be relevant. Finally, remember that at this deepening layer of dream exploration, your search for meaning may take you far afield from the original content of the dream itself.

Eight

DREAMS, CREATIVITY, AND HEALING JOURNEYS

"What if you slept? And what if in your sleep,
you dreamed? And what if, in your dream,
you went to heaven and plucked a strange
and beautiful flower? And what if, when you
awoke, you had the flower in your hand? Ah,
what then?"
Samuel Taylor Coleridge

Some of our most creative work comes through in that genera-
tive sweet spot in the still of the night and depths of our dreams.
In that quiet place at 3:00 a.m., we can feel a quality of hushed
holiness permeate our being while the rest of the world sleeps.
In her blog at carlagolembe.com, artist Carla Golembe writes,
"My paintings are the product of my dreams and experiences...

133

My work expresses the harmony between individuals, between people and animals, people and nature within a person's soul ... the figures often inhabit ambiguous spaces, places where earth, sky and water flow into one another and where light and darkness merge. They are frequently caught in a moment of being or becoming, for it is in that moment that all dreams are possible." A prolific artist, Carla frequently uses her dreams as source material. Her paintings have a dreamlike quality at times reminiscent of another artist who used dreams as source material, Marc Chagall.

Creativity encompasses the ability to transcend traditional ideas, rules, and patterns, and to then create meaningful new forms or connections. It involves originality, imagination, and the ability to think outside the box. These elements of our creative process point toward the gifts from both the nocturnal and waking dream states as wonderful resources to enhance our creative life. In one of her monthly newsletters, Victoria Rabinowe, artist and dreamworker, writes, "Out of this realm of mystery and paradox, a wellspring of inspiration opens up."

To access our creativity we need a sufficient supply of energy and resources. If our well is dry, we can't get water from it. When mine ran dry, resupplying it took me several weeks of vacation and sufficient solitude. Our creative wellspring can run dry for many reasons: overwork, stress, worry, illness, lack of sleep, lack of meaningful deep sleep, and simply the "too much-ness" of our plugged-in everyday lives. It is a chronic modern problem.

Before gas and electricity lit up the night, to say nothing of our ubiquitous computer screens, people went to bed when the sun went down. They naturally wound down as darkness fell and settled into first sleep (lasting a few hours), followed by a normal nocturnal wakeful period. There inside the deep early morning silence they could think, muse, and easily remember their dreams. They would rest in this soft fertile space, possibly chat quietly with their partner, meditate, or wander in thought until they naturally nodded off again into the second sleep, which lasted until morning light. This was the norm for pre-industrial society.

I was relieved when I learned about this concept, as I often wake in the night and don't fall right back to sleep. The book *World Enough and Time: On Slowing Down and Creativity* by Christian McEwen enlightened me to this pattern of first and second sleeps. Her book is so beautifully written that I initially ignored the directive of the title and quickly devoured it. Later I followed the advice of slowing down and enjoyed a second slow and savory read.

Countless authors, musicians, and scientists have credited their dreams with providing answers and creative ideas, and reported using this still time of the night after the first sleep for creativity. Author Robert Louis Stevenson's dream muse supplied him with the story of *Dr. Jekyll and Mr. Hyde*; Mozart often woke late at night and composed music; Gaughan painted. Computer scientist and futurist Ray Kurzweil uses the time for his creative work.

Next time you wake in the night, you might try using the time for creativity if you haven't already. You may "dream through" into breakthroughs in this fertile time, once your common anxiety about being awake quiets.

Dreaming as Creative Problem-Solving

The phrase "let me sleep on it" has real value. We know that while we are asleep our brain functions are different than when we are awake. During sleep our left analytical brain goes mostly off-line, and our less linear and more imaginative right brain goes more on-line. We have more access to thinking outside the box while asleep and can dream up options that we would not have considered while awake. Many of us do wonderfully outrageous things in our dreams that we would not "dream of" doing in our waking lives. Thankfully, our internal censor is asleep as well, so we can try things out that our waking rule-follower may have not allowed.

When we incubate dreams, the more specific the question we ask, the greater the likelihood that we will receive a correspondingly specific response from the dream universe. This is true for our creative questions as well as life's other dilemmas and mysteries.

If you are stuck on writing that next part of your novel, you can ask your dream muse for more than simply to "get unstuck." Be specific. Don't just ask for inspiration—ask for it with specificity. For example, if your novel explores time travel, ask specifically how to invite the reader to easily suspend their disbelief and embrace your character as she travels from the twentieth century in America to ancient Egypt and then to the deep jungles of the Amazon at the turn of the century. Or for the artist, "What exact shades of blue do I need for my palate to make the water shimmer in my painting?" Or for the poet, "I am trying to create a sense of spaciousness and movement in this next section of my poem. What words will help me do that?"

Dream Resources for Our Creative Process

We can draw water from our creative dream-well from three main sources: the narrative story of the dream itself, the emotions within the dream, and the images and pictures in the dream. These three elements let us attend to the verbal message or storyline of the dream, the feelings in different parts of the dream and how they impact our project—be it a writing project, an art project, an invention, or a creative solution to a life conundrum. The messages include what transpired inside the dream itself, as well as what comes through in the post-dream exploration.

Rabinowe says, "Dreams have a voice and a presence of their own ... My role is to create a space in which [we] can enter the living experience of [our] own dreams." This echoes the teaching that living dream images have an *a priori* life of their own. In addition to writing down our dreams, we can create a welcoming space for them by embodying them, drawing or painting them, acting them out, dialoguing with them, dancing them, or making poetry out of them. Dreams and poetry share a common language of image, metaphor, and association as well as a non-attachment to the rules of logic, grammar, and time sequence. It's no wonder that dreams are a frequent source of inspiration for poets from Walt Whitman to Mary Oliver.

Let's start with story, creative dream resource number one. Our dreams usually come through with some kind of storyline. It may be a very short story (the equivalent of a sentence or two), a full-length narrative, or even an epic. We can examine our dream story for its personal meaning (healing, problem-solving, a spiritual quest, etc.) and also as a freestanding story in its own right.

Look for elements like the major plotline, the dynamic tensions and relationships between the characters, the sources of conflict, and whether or not they were resolved. You can also examine the dream to see if an inner or outer journey was involved.

Studying our dream in this way can help turn our dream story into art. Does our dream connect us with a larger mythos, as the dreams of the two tents did? A consultant of mine introduced me to a self-actualization concept: "I am the story I tell myself I am." What is the story your psyche wants told? Think back for a moment to Jana's dreams about the two tents. There is a plotline of tents not protecting or not being suitable, the characters in the second dream are annoying but also carry advice, and the outer journey of wandering in the desert is reflected by the inner journey of the "desert" of her current creative and marital landscape.

Authors tell us that inspirations for their stories can come from their dreams. In 1816, at a party of assorted authors at Lord Byron's house, guest Mary (Wollstonecraft) Shelley proposed a competition to see who could write the best horror story. The creative crowd liked this idea. Earlier that evening they had been discussing the possibility of re-animating a corpse with electricity, giving it what they called "vital warmth." That night Mary had a terrifying dream integrating this idea with one about a scientist who creates a new man and then assumes the role of God. This tale "haunted my midnight pillow," says Shelley, and went far beyond the parlor of Lord Byron's house to become known the world over as *Frankenstein*.

Shelley said she needed only to make a transcript of her dream to have her story.

Using Dream Story to Create a Healing Journey:

Creative engagement with our dreams can also serve as a tool to heal and transform our lives. According to biographer Katharine M. Rogers, as a child *The Wizard of Oz* author L. Frank Baum had nightmares of a scarecrow chasing him and trying to put its fingers around his neck. He later gained mastery over that nightmare when he reimagined and reintegrated the scarecrow figure into a benevolent and gentle helper for Dorothy.

Baum's solution of transforming a frightening dream character into a source of help and wisdom exemplifies how we can rewrite our dream stories to gain a new and more satisfying resolution to them. We can also restructure dialogues between characters, resolve tensions in the dream, and add resources that our dream characters need inside the dream itself.

You might creatively engage with the dream by, for example, turning left at a crossroads instead of turning right, and imagining how the story changes as a result. If that crossroads is where a car rammed you because you turned left, you might avoid the collision by turning right instead. Instead of drowning when the ship capsizes, what would happen if you were able to call your dolphin allies at that moment to carry you to safety? These rewritten dream stories could then become part of your new life story, the basis for an artistic project, or a new source of healing. In narrative therapy, this is a technique known as "spotlighting." We highlight, or spotlight, the positive or the potential positive, and find the silver thread to pull from the dream of darkness or confusion to reweave the dreamscape with bright new thread. The following anecdote is an example of beginning to transform a nightmare into a healing journey.

While I was vacationing at our annual dance camp, laying on the beach by the lake and letting the warm sun relax my sore muscles before my next class, another dancer, Debra, approached me, saying, "I heard that you do dreamwork. I've had a really bizarre dream. Could you listen to it?" I told her that I only had about twenty minutes free just then, but agreed to listen and do what I could in that amount of time. You will see why Debra felt an urgency to address her dream. She said that in her dream she wants to break up with her boyfriend, who is good to her, but really boring. She leaves him and tries to get home, but gets lost on a street in New York City. As she walks around looking for her way home she meets a man when she asks for directions. He says that he will give them to her if she goes up to his apartment with him first to get them. She goes up, and then he tells her that he will not let her leave, and he is planning to sell her into slavery. Then she woke up with her heart pounding.

Not what I was expecting to hear while lying on the beach. Given the intense content of this dream, I told Debra that this felt like an important dream that deserved more time than I had just then, but that I would be willing to give it what I could, as long as we both acknowledged that it would be incomplete. As a dreamworker and therapist, having heard this, I felt a responsibility to respond in at least a limited fashion. I also checked to be sure she had resources available at camp (such as a supportive friend or family member), given the storyline of being lost and then held captive.

I began working with her dream by asking her for a title. This simple yet powerful first step has many benefits, one being that it provides a way to track the dreamwork and see if the title changes after we work on the dream. When a title does change, it can mean the dreamer has made some headway in resolving the underlying issue or dilemma. Debra's first title summed up her thoughts and feelings about the dream in one word: "Trapped." Next, to track the emotional content of the dream for resonance with her life, I asked if the dream accurately expresses her feelings about her boyfriend. Debra responds yes, he is "safe" but they have little in common and she is bored with him.

I now invite her to go back to the dream, asking her where she can make a different choice or do something different in order to obtain a different ending. Debra replies that she wants to change the dream when the story takes her up to the apartment of the man she meets on the street. My instincts, intuition, clinical experience, and just common sense tell me that this might be too late, so I ask if that is where she *first* started to feel unsafe in the dream.

A core concept for work on upsetting dreams is to establish or reestablish safety. Ideally, we want to start the dreamwork where the dreamer does feel safe and has resources, and build from there, rather than starting where she doesn't feel safe. We'll cover this in more detail in chapter 11 on nightmares. I asked her how she felt down on the street when the man first made that suggestion for her to go up to his apartment, and she realized that was actually where she began to get anxious and nervous, but she went up anyway. My query was not intended to impose my choice on her, but to make an observation that she was free to use or discard. Given her response, I asked her if she could make a different choice while on the street, before going up to his apartment, since that is where I felt that the dream turned into nightmare territory. She immediately said, "I could tell him no thanks, I'll get directions from someone else, and then walk away. There are plenty of other people on the streets of New York who could help me out."

Debra confirmed that this choice felt right, so I encouraged her now to rework the dream. I invited her to re-enter the dreamscape, then walk away from that man and get directions home from a safe person (back toward *home* is key; that's where she was trying to go in her original dream). Once she had done this and was safely on the road home, I invited her to repeat her dream action three times. Three is the magic number not only in fairy tales, but also in dream rehearsal, in order to better create a new neural imprint in our brains. After she performed her dream action three times, I asked if she had a new title. She replied yes: "Independence." We agreed that progressing from "Trapped" to

"Independence" was pretty good for twenty minutes of dream-work; maybe even very, very good! We spotlighted her ability to make a healthy choice and use her skills of differentiation to choose a better directional guide.

By making a different choice at that crucial juncture of the dream, Debra re-storied an ongoing theme of powerlessness in her life, which she had shared with me in background material about her life's current circumstances. She also discovered options other than being stuck between boredom and endangerment. If she does break up with her boyfriend in the dream, she may feel lost for a while, but does not have to follow a stranger up to his apartment to get directions. In other words, she has other options both in the dream and in her life. By making a different choice in the dream, she primed the pump for making a different choice in her life. I was careful to stay just in the dream material and not move out of the dream into her life in this brief encounter. She was not my therapy client. When we make shifts in our dream story, we are making shifts in our self-story. That one will be Debra's own journey to make.

The Emotional Story

In addition to the storyline and the images, there are emotions that accompany them, often rising up from deep in our unconscious selves to emerge in the dreamscape. The emotional narrative is perhaps the most important element in dreamwork. When our limbic system—which is our emotional brain—is calm, we too are at peace in our bodies and our souls.

Next let's look at creative dream resource number two, the emotional story of our dream. Sometimes the emotional storyline is congruent to the dream narrative; sometimes it seems surprisingly out of sync. There is a felt sense that the words and the music don't match. We would expect to feel fear if we were about to be sold into slavery as in Debra's dream—it would be incongruent with the story if we didn't have a strong emotional reaction. If we didn't, that would be an important detail to notice during the dreamwork. However, there might be a variety of emotional responses to dreaming about breaking up with a boyfriend or girlfriend (sadness, relief, ambivalence), or going up to someone's apartment (curiosity, trepidation, excitement). Whether the emotion is what one would expect to feel, or it is quite different, it can be a strong indicator that there are layers to plumb here to get at the deeper meaning.

The most important indicators of the meaning of your dreams are the emotions felt within and immediately following the dream. The emotional resonance of the dream within the context of your life provides the core of meaning that makes this "my dream," as opposed to "anyone's dream."

We feel our emotions in our bodies. They are called feelings because we actually *feel* them. Notice your physical responses to the emotions in your dreams. Pay attention to where in your body you have a sensation, and what it feels like. Is it in your chest, your belly, or your fingers, for example. Is it agitated, peaceful, tight, hard, constricted, warm, tingly? This is the *felt sense* of the dream. Our physical responses resonate in us at a level that bypasses our analyzing and thinking brain, thus containing an unmediated core of inner truth and integrity. Tuning in to the emotions and sensations in our dreams enhances and informs creativity: our poetry, our dance, the characters in our novel, the decision we have to make about a project at work, our self-narratives, and so forth.

Dance and movement are avenues of allowing the body to express the felt sense of a dream. Dance to express the dreamed emotions; act out the sensations; let them move through you physically. When you embody the emotion you discover new dimensions of the dream. Engage your friends, your family, or your dream circle to act out a scene from your dream. Previously we spoke of embodying the image; now try embodying a dream scene or character to tune into the emotional story that emerges. Our emotional resonance and body sensations can provide another yellow brick road to follow on the path to understanding our dreams.

Dancer and choreographer Martha Graham created a dance piece called Lamentation. In it, she takes the visceral emotion of grief and embodies it in powerful images on the stage. A solo dancer is clad in a tube-like lavender garment with only her face, hands, and bare feet showing. She does not dance *about* grief as much as she embodies and *becomes* grief. She uses the stretchy fabric as a second skin, one that she appears to want to break free of. As we watch, we feel alongside her the pain, the anguish, and the deep sorrow that are felt very strongly while grieving. Graham wanted her dances to be felt, not just seen. These emotional stories that are embedded in our dreams and lives can be tapped for creative resources as Graham did, as well as for our own healing journeys. While we don't know the source of Graham's dance piece, we can see in her dance this embodiment of emotion. We too can use this embodied emotional information for healing and catharsis when the emotion comes through from one of our dreams.

The Visual Images

The images in our dreams—creative resource number three—provide perhaps the richest source of inspiration for visual arts.

You can draw the images, paint them, or collect found objects that call to you while focusing on your dream and then make a montage or a shadow box of them. Pick one moment from the dream to capture, or use the dream as a whole. Try not to let artistic talent that you do or don't believe you have get in the way of making a representation of your dream. I usually draw stick figures when drawing people in my dreams; they serve the purpose just fine. Mara, a client of mine, cut pictures out of magazines to make a montage of her images and associations to her dream, finding a new layer of comfort in literally manipulating the images.

You might try finding objects to create a scene from your dream. Different objects can represent different characters, locations, or emotions. For example, a yellowed or crumbling autumn leaf represents the passage of time, a stick stuck in the ground represents feeling stuck, a smooth stone represents calm peaceful feelings, a spray of bittersweet represents your parents. You can use shells, tree bark, flowers, feathers, twine, bottle caps—whatever is readily available. Remember to let yourself be surprised.

Victoria Rabinowe reminds us that an important aspect of translating a dream with found objects is the serendipity (similar to synchronicity) of what you find. Sit and contemplate what you have created. Then you may write or create a dialogue between the objects that represent the characters, the emotions, or the landscapes in the dream; or speak with the voice of the objects you have chosen, to provide a new dimension to your dream and your creative process. Go back and forth between what you are creating and what the dream has brought you as each enriches the other. Have fun with it.

In addition to the three main dream sources of story, emotion, and image for our creative muse, there are other additional sources as well. One may be our association to place—the dream's location, topography, landscape, or features. Another source may be a particular character or the interactions between characters in your dream. That might even prompt dialogue for characters if you are writing a play or book.

You can also find inspiration in what emerges when you title the dream, and what happens when you practice dream re-entry and move around inside the dream. Perhaps most importantly for our creative selves, the specific action plan you formulate and then use to move your dream into the world will bring it to life.

Color-Full Dreams

In one of his many letters to his brother Theo, Vincent van Gogh wrote, "I dream my paintings, and then I paint my dreams." Artist Carla Golembe finds many of the vivid colors of her palate in her dreams. Our brains are hardwired to resonate emotionally with different colors, so when color shows up in a dream it has the potential to connect us to both the narrative and the emotional storylines. We don't always notice whether or not we dream in color unless something jumps out at us as we are writing or remembering the dream. As we recall the dream, we may be struck suddenly by a color we hadn't noticed previously.

A large, very bright blue stone showed up in one of my dreams, as the central image. This color blue and the symbol of the stone then graced my dreams off and on for years until I took the needed actions that the stone was prompting me toward (stay tuned for the dream and the healing journey story). We have already learned to pay attention when dream imagery reoccurs. That prompting applies to recurring colors, too. Uncovering the significance of the colors in your dreams can add another layer of emotional resonance that may otherwise be missed or misinterpreted.

Now, do the following mini-exercise.

Close your eyes and see the feathery chartreuse yellow-green color of newly emerging leaves tinged with wispy pink blossoms, like one of Nick Zungali's photographs in soft focus.

See a brilliant, two-inch long blue stone, a cross between a lapis and a turquoise, shimmering with the turquoise blue of the Caribbean and the cobalt blue Adriatic seas, set in finely wrought silver filigree.

See the silver bullet of a plane, hard and metallic, leaving a trail of white herringbone tail feathers across the orange and pink sunset sky.

Whether you are painting or dancing or describing with words, these colors from dreams add a rich dimension to your creative pursuits. They add emotional resonance, a focal point calling attention. "Look at me! Don't miss this!" When an otherwise nondescript color scheme in a dream suddenly pops with a notable splash of color, it's often pointing our attention to a central image in the dream.

In Oz and during Dorothy's journey home, color plays a key role several times. The slippers that Dorothy wears are pointedly ruby red, not green or blue or some other color. In fact, the shoes in the original story were silver, but the movie directors decided that red would pop more vividly against the yellow bricks. The emerald city is quite clearly green, as is the skin tone of its residents. And the road to follow on our journey is yellow. It twists and turns and goes through the dark brown woods and the field of red poppies all the way to the Wizard.

We all have our own associations with these colors. At a neurological level, the color red excites our autonomic nervous system, and can fire us up with associations to danger, excitement, and/or passion. The color blue calms the autonomic nervous system, and is associated with serenity, calm, and peacefulness. Robert Hoss, author of *Dream Language: Self-Understanding Through Imagery and Color*, points out that all this associating happens below the threshold of our awareness, yet has a profound effect on our emotional state.

In addition to universal or instinctive responses to colors, an extensive set of cultural and personal associations to colors is ingrained in our subconscious. Hoss reminds us that these associations come from our myths, our literature, our families, our language, our personal histories, and our cultures. Therefore, paying attention to the colors in your dreams not only adds emotional richness to your understanding, but can significantly affect the meanings you make out of them.

EXERCISE

Make a color wheel of your personal associations with a color found in one or several of your dreams. Using the sun and spokes drawing method, without self-censoring or thinking about the actual dream image, just write down your associations to the color itself. For example, when I think of yellow, I make my circle and write the words canary, yellow-bellied (cowardice), cheerful, sunshine, the yellow brick road, bright, and jaundiced. I then go back to the yellow dream image and circle the associations I wrote down that somehow seem related to this dream. You can see how dreaming of a yellow sweater would have a very different meaning if the associations to yellow were of cheerful and bright, as opposed to cowardly or sickly.

Below is an abridged version of the Luscher Color Association chart, a psychological profiling tool that matches colors with some of their common emotional responses. It is not a complete list of all associations to colors; rather it is a good starting point for connecting emotional overtones to colors in your dreams. You can add your own personal associations as you build up your own repertoire. The list does not include non-Western cultural associations, such as red being associated with a wedding dress in India and China, or white as associated with widows or death.

> *Red:* active, aggressive, joy, passion, danger, power, hot, "stop"
>
> *Orange:* friendly, warm, active, enthusiastic, autumn, harvest
>
> *Yellow:* cheerful, spontaneous, alert, positive, prosperity, "caution"
>
> *Green:* nature, youthfulness, spring, growth, money, safety, "go"
>
> *Blue:* calm, serenity, fulfillment, tranquility, unity, tenderness, sadness
>
> *Violet/Purple:* royalty, mystic union, sensitivity, sensuality, luxury, magic
>
> *Brown:* earth, comfort, warmth, roots, dirty
>
> *Grey:* uncommitted, uninvolved, shielding of self, sadness

Black: evil, badness, nothingness, extinction, shadow
side, unknown

White: purity, innocence, peace, light, goodness,
holiness

Pink: romantic, love, soft, gentleness

Gold/Silver: the sun and moon, value, psychological
integration, wealth

Now, with some of this background material in mind, we return to my blue stone—the two-inch long stone that had been following me around for years in my dreams. It brought to my mind associations with the mythic sorcerer's stone, with the breastplate of High Priest Aaron (Moses's brother) and its twelve gemstones that could be used for divination, and with the blue of deep seas and deep emotions. My dream compelled me to search for this stone in my waking life—it was the task I gave myself in response to the powerful pull and the ubiquitous nature of this dream image. One time I ordered a necklace from a picture in a catalogue that seemed very similar to the dream stone. After it arrived in the mail I realized that although it was pretty, it was not *my* stone. I could enjoy wearing it, but it had no special significance.

Several years after the original dream I finally found my stone in the Shuk, a marketplace in the Old City of Jerusalem. While poking in and out of small storefronts on one of the narrow, winding streets, I came across an array of jewelry and there it was: a turquoise/blue/lapis stone set in a filigree of silver. I found it on the same trip to Israel when I reclaimed a lost part of myself, as I discussed earlier.

Finding my *true stone* brought all the pieces together. It's the "true blue" of unification, pulling together parts of my life that had become separated. It's the blue that embodies my associations with deep emotions and personal fulfillment. It carries mystical qualities associated with divination, connecting me with Aaron and further with the land and history of Israel. I wear that necklace often, especially when doing dreamwork.

EXERCISE

This chapter included a number of suggestions of exercises to try out. If you haven't already done so, try working with a dream by expressing it artistically. What does your dream want from you—to be danced, painted, acted out, or handled in another way that expresses your uniqueness? Ask the dream. Draw a sketch based on a dream image; childlike drawings are fine. Make yourself a color wheel. Collect objects to make a montage. Do you have an artistic project that could use an extra *zetz*? Try incubating a dream for that purpose, remembering to be as specific as possible in your request.

Does a particular color pop for you in a dream? What are your associations with it? Go beyond whether you like the color or not, or whether you would ever wear it. If you are not a red-wearing person but are wearing red in a dream, that may be significant too. Let your associations take you out beyond the dream itself to see where they are pointing you. Investigate how the reaction you have to this color is relevant to your dream and your life.

What are your emotional resonances to all the parts of a dream? I often create the emotional narrative section by leaving a bit of room on the page as

I write the dream down, and then placing a vertical line next to the dream and writing the corresponding emotions on the other side of it. As you write out the feeling narrative alongside the action or storyline, see if there are places where you could rework the dream action to achieve a different and more positive emotional resonance. This is particularly powerful with upsetting dreams or nightmares. If you have titled your dream before working on it, what title does it now have once you have changed your dream action in some way, thus altering your emotional response?

Nine

THE ANIMALS AND THE PEOPLE IN OUR DREAMS

"The animals which are our totems are
mirrors to us. They reflect lessons we need
to learn and abilities we can most easily
develop ... [They are] a medicine for healing
yourself and your life, and a power that can
be accessed to help manifest your dreams."
Ted Andrews

Animals frequently show up in our dreams. An owl may ask, "Who, who, who?" Who comes calling? Is it friend or foe? What do our nocturnal visitors mean or want from us? People who we know, as well as random strangers, populate our dreams. Our dearly (or not so dearly) departed relatives show up in our dreams, which raises the question of whether these are actual visitations from the Other Side, or a metaphor for something else. It may be a haunting, or a gift, or a symbol. We are meant to learn something from the people and animals that appear in our dreams, and the messages may vary depending on the dream and the context.

Dorothy had several beings as companions on her mythic journey through Oz, including her "familiar" Toto. A familiar is a concept for an animal that is part of your soul-self, and frequently accompanies you through life. Witches are commonly portrayed as having a cat as their familiar, hence the ubiquitous image of a cat riding the broomstick along with the witch on Halloween. Interestingly, Toto is the only companion who travels with Dorothy as himself on both sides of the rainbow in both Kansas and Oz. Her other Kansas friends and neighbors show up in symbolic form in Oz. If Toto is her familiar, a part of her soul-self, then they need to be together in both realms.

Dorothy meets the Scarecrow, the Tin Man, and the Cowardly Lion as guides and companions on her journey. She needs the qualities they symbolically embody—wisdom, heart, and courage—to complete her hero's journey and return home. At first these characters seem to embody the opposite of the qualities they later are known to carry: your typical scarecrow has his head stuffed with straw rather than wisdom, the Tin Man tells us that his maker forgot to give him a heart, and our Lion is just a big 'fraidy cat until much later in the story. Part of this hero's journey for her companions, as well as for Dorothy herself, is to come into the fullness of their potential and reclaim their buried strengths.

Animals and the Paradox of Opposites: Our Shadow Side

This inside-out representation of Dorothy's three companions is another aspect of our "shadows," those darker sides of ourselves that need to be redeemed. Inside-out, upside-down, Mobius strip twisting, "through the looking glass," "down the rabbit hole"— these are all realms of the dream universe, and of the shadow side in particular. In our dreams, the beings of our shadow sides often initially show up as animals or characters of diminished qualities or of malevolence. Our shadow contains our unconscious urges and the qualities that we hide even (or especially) from ourselves. They are the hidden parts of ourselves that we are embarrassed or ashamed of. The shadow in our dreams brings us face to face with our undeveloped parts, containing the seeds of our redemption if we engage with them. Our shadow teachers show us both our limits and our potential.

We need to traverse these darker realms to emerge into the light. "We're out of the dark, we're out of the woods, we're into the light…" Dorothy and her companions sang this after leaving the forest and getting their first glimpse of Oz. Little did they know at that point in their journey that there were darker woods yet to come as they neared the witch's lair. Sometimes we think we've got it all figured out, but then…

Healing and integration occur when we are no longer projecting our dark sides onto others, and we are able to integrate all parts of ourselves. We read previously that Jung said, "We do not become enlightened by imagining figures of light, but by making the darkness conscious." The rest of this quote continues, "This latter procedure, however, is disagreeable and therefore not popular." How true. Few people I know voluntarily examine their darkest sides unless forced to by outside circumstances.

In *The Wizard of Oz*, Dorothy's companions show up first in their diminished shadow sides. Only as the story progresses do they grow to reveal the full potential of their inner nature. When we first meet the straw-stuffed, "empty-headed" Scarecrow, he claims that he has no brain. He stumbles and trips and can't seem to tell his right from his left. Yet time and again he is the one who gives Dorothy the wisest counsel. The "empty-chested" Tin Man is the one who holds the heart center, the tears, and the compassion for the group, and our scaredy-cat Cowardly Lion finally finds his courage when it is most needed—when he is most afraid.

This embodies the definition of courage. Courage does not mean to be fearless, but rather to move forward in spite of our fear. Our "animal instincts" may be part of our more primitive selves (our instinctual lower brain is even called our "reptilian brain" in neuroscience texts), yet we could not survive without our instincts. The dark and the light together unify the whole. To receive the gifts of our shadow characters (including the wickedest of witches) requires a willingness and ability to embrace this paradox.

Lion and Tigers and Bears and Snakes and Owls and Unicorns: Animals in Our Dreams

Animals are among our most common dream images. They can delight, scare, intrigue, or puzzle us when they show up in our dreams, and they contain some of the most complex layers of universal and personal symbolism. Our "animal selves" contain the purest expressions of our emotions and psyches. When we react to sudden danger, our instinctive reptilian brains go into fight or flight mode, and if we are lucky or skilled or both, our animal instincts keep us safe. When a saber-toothed tiger or a marauder is approaching, we have no time to reason or bargain. We need to act fast, and that means act from our animal instincts. One layer of meaning or symbolism of animals in a dream can be about our primitive instincts. We can study the basic nature of the animal that we are dreaming about (that *a priori* nature) to discern the connection to its meaning and presence in our dream. As always, we need to contextualize the meaning of the animal that appears in our dreams to understand it within the content of the whole dream, the emotions we experience in response to it, and the nature of it.

Many native and indigenous peoples put great stock in animal visitations. They believe that the spirit of the animal has meaning or a message for our lives. In fact, if we frequently dream of the same animal, it may be our "spirit" animal—a sort of guide or guardian whose qualities we should learn about and perhaps embody. A totem is a spirit-animal helper. The root of the word is from the native Ojibway, also known as the Chippewa, from the upper Great Lakes region, meaning "brother/sister kin."

My go-to guy on the meaning of animal symbols in dreams is Ted Andrews. In his classic book *Animal Speak*, Andrews teaches that our relationship with animals exists not only in the physical world, but in the spiritual or mystical one as well. He combines mythology and factual information to help us learn about and tune into the essence of the animal who shows up in our lives or our dreams. My universal caution regarding other people's opinions about what your dream or symbol means applies to everyone's opinion, including Andrews's—it's only true for you if it resonates with you. Your dream, your cat, your symbolic meanings.

Andrews gives us a great number of potential associations to connect with, including mythological references, behaviors of animals in the wild, prey and predator relationships, seasonal representations, and the "keynote" or core message of each animal. Jamie Sams, in the book *Medicine Cards*, provides a description of many animal totems, and an accompanying deck of cards to pull as one might use a tarot deck, used to find waking dream messages, as well as to look up the animals that appeared in your dream. Shamanic teachers Sandra Ingerman and Lynn Robert in their book, *Speaking with Nature: Awakening to the Deep Wisdom of the Earth*, add an additional perspective by tapping into the feminine side of animals and nature teachings. They echo some of Clarissa Pinkola Estés's work previously discussed by applying a feminine viewpoint to Andrew's more traditional teaching. There are many authors who can provide us with source material for the meaning of the animals that inhabit our dreams.

Here are a few examples of animals that appear in our dreams with multifaceted potential meanings, followed by a few mythological examples. I encourage you to utilize the work of Andrews and others to further explore what these and other animals are coming to show and tell you in your dreams and in your daytime sightings.

Cat

If a cat named Tammy shows up in your dream, is she your own beloved cat, a random cat with that name, or the "cat from hell"? Might you be exhausted in your life and in need of sleeping eighteen hours a day in a warm, sunny spot? The answers to these types of considerations and questions will lead you to the important meaning.

Next, use a wider-angle lens to expand your view of the broader category of cats, seeing them both as pets and as creatures of the wild. Consider the general characteristics of the animal and, if the animal is a pet, also consider specific characteristics of your cat. Cats in general are known to be curious, clever, and independent, and those characteristics could be the basis of the symbolism. When the animal is one you know personally, your dream associations may be more specific, based on your personal knowledge and relationship with them. Your personal pet Tammy may be cuddly, or aloof, or attached to you like a puppy dog (as my cat Effie is), or keep you awake all night with her yowling. This insider information gives you specific associations to work with while interpreting. Tammy could even be a friend or relative's pet, and used in the dream to refer to its owner, as in "Tammy is my sister's cat, and when I think of my sister …"

Snake

For millennia, the snake has been the subject of controversy and paradox. It's seen as both the highest and the lowest of symbols—blamed for the downfall of mankind in the Garden of Eden, but held up as a symbol of death and rebirth, as well as of renewal for its ability to shed its outgrown skin time after time.

The snake eating its own tail is the symbol of the ouroboros, endlessly reincarnating and symbolizing eternity. It is the symbol of healing powers in the entwined caduceus of medicine. The snake can also be a phallic symbol of sexuality or fertility, and is the symbol of creative kundalini energy in Eastern traditions.

When a snake shows up in your dreams, it might mean that some kind of death and rebirth or healing may be happening or may be needed in a part of your life. This is not necessarily an actual death, but perhaps the death of an outmoded belief or way of being, and an opening for something new.

In the book of Exodus, God tells Moses that the people will be healed when they look upon his snake-entwined staff after they were bitten by deadly vipers. This image has become the prototype for our modern caduceus. This story contains a deep shamanic teaching. When we transform and face our poison and our fears we become healed rather than killed by them. A tiny drop of a poison is actually what is used in a homeopathic remedy. In this very diluted form the poison itself becomes the remedy.

We build up immunity when exposed to a drop of certain types of poison. We are healed when we look upon something reminiscent of prior danger (such as Moses's staff reminding us of the previous live deadly snakes). Our dreams can expose us to our fears, and we can heal when we metabolize and learn from the message.

Owl

The owl is known as a symbol of the feminine and of the night, an animal friend frequently associated with sleep and dreams, magic, the secrets the darkness has to offer, and the transition to the other side after death. This ability for keen vision and hearing may also be why owls are also symbolic of knowledge and wisdom. Athena, the Greek goddess of wisdom, is often depicted with her owl companion.

I have had two owl visitations. One was the barred owl I wrote about in chapter 4 that visited me on my writing retreat at ten o'clock in the morning; the other was in a night dream. This second owl came to me the night after my dad had undergone complicated and risky surgery. I sensed right away that it meant he was going to transition over, but I argued with myself, not wanting it to be true, saying, "Oh, owls can have many meanings." I was right though, and he died shortly thereafter. I am convinced that the owl came to help me prepare for his passing. I was less taken by surprise than I might have been without that visitation.

Mythological Animal Beings

Waking reality does not limit our dream guides, and animal or animal-like beings from myth, fairy tale, and legend may appear as well. A "Big Bad Wolf" or an "Ugly Duckling" or a "Golden Goose" may appear in your dreams or your life. Your dream may contain a centaur, a unicorn, or a mermaid. Or you may dream about a minotaur (the Greek bull-headed man/beast in the middle of the Labyrinth on Crete), a sphinx (the Egyptian creature with the head of a pharaoh and the body of a lion), or a phoenix (an ancient symbol of renewal and rebirth, predating Dumbledore's companion/familiar/alter ego in the Harry Potter series). Like Dumbledore's, the phoenix is a shimmering mythological bird that lives for centuries, and when it dies in flames, it is then reborn out of its own ashes.

Track your own dream animals back to the myths and archetypes (our collective inheritance of images, stories, and larger-than-life figures such as the wise old man or woman, the witch, or the trickster). Find their larger resonance for yourself in our mythic patterns and our collective unconscious where, according to Jung, ancestral memories and experiences are housed deep within our own unconscious minds. These deep and universal archetypes can then take you even farther along the road to your truest self, because your dream exploration will then include aspects of the deep story or myth with which your personal dreams resonate. In my dream about the resplendent quetzal, it was *my* dream bird that flew in through the window, but the bird also echoed and resonated with the mythological associations from the ancient Maya that were stored in *our* collective unconscious.

We must also examine the *a priori* nature of our dream animals and characters, as well as their potential symbolic meanings. In other words, what are the real world qualities of the images we dream about, regardless of how they show up in our dream? What actually is a scarecrow, or a lion, or a pet dog—what are their qualities, their attributes, their purposes? A scarecrow, for example, is usually a figure of a man made out of straw, which is placed in a cornfield for the purpose of scaring away crows and other birds that may eat the crops. They function as protection for the farmers and for all who will eat the crops of the field. So at another level, we might also understand a dream scarecrow as a protector of our sustenance or nourishment.

The Other Side of the Veil: Our Dear Departed Ones

In *Fiddler on the Roof*, Tevye needs to convince his wife Golde that they should break with tradition and allow their daughter Tzeitel to marry her beloved Motel the tailor, rather than Lazar Wolf, to whom she was betrothed. To get his wife to agree to this plan, he pretends that Goldie's beloved deceased grandma had appeared to him in a dream to give her blessing to this new idea of a love match. Tevye knew the power of dreams for his wife, and that a dream visit with a message from the other side would have an unarguable impact on her. So, taking no chances, in his fabricated dream scene, Tevye wakes up Goldie and reports what he had been "told" in a dream by her grandma that she is giving her blessing to the match. Tevye's ploy of reporting visits from beyond the grave finally convinced Goldie of the validity of this newfangled plan of marrying for love.

If we suspend our own disbelief at the possibility of multiple realities, we can experience great comfort and connection when our departed beloveds visit us in our dream worlds. Many people who have lost a loved one say that they have had a sense that their dad or grandma or other loved one visited them in a dream, but they weren't sure whether to believe it. Or they say that they wish they could have a visit, and wonder why mom hasn't shown up yet. My first suggestion when I hear someone express the desire for a loved one's visitation is usually to ask if they have offered the beloved an invitation or request yet. Spiritual energy beings seem to be like cats—they have lives of their own (pun intended) and may not come when we call.

My first dream visitation from a departed beloved actually came from my cat Ashorka. She came to visit in a dream I had a few months after her death. In it, she assured me that she was happy and would be a guide to me when my time came to cross over as well. She was one of the lucky ones—she died peacefully in her sleep at the ripe old cat age of sixteen years. She is my role model for a good death. I referred to her as a grey Buddha in a fur suit, and her name actually came to me in a dream about a cat gazing deeply into my eyes when we first brought her home from the shelter. She was frequently my co-therapist and would slip down to my office and do therapy with me. She seemed to have an innate understanding of who needed their leg rubbed or a warm, furry visitor in their lap at just the right moment.

I wonder if it is easier for animals to cross over these thresholds, since they do not seem limited by our view of what is "real" or not. And perhaps the animals and their people continue to share a soul connection after they depart, as well as in life (as in the "familiar" that we referenced previously). After my dad died, my mom reported that a bright red male cardinal knocked at her bedroom window each night for several evenings, an event that had never occurred before, or since. Whenever we see a cardinal now we always say "Hi, Dad."

Cultural traditions in places like Tibet and ancient Egypt speak of a time after death when the spirit of the departed needs to get used to the afterlife before being ready to visit the earth plane. They may be hanging out in the *bardo*, that in-between place that's neither here nor there, and consequently may be unready to visit us until they're more fully settled on the other side. My instincts tell me to give them at least a few weeks to get settled after the death of their body before requesting a visit.

Visit or Symbol?

Having departed friends or family members show up in a dream indicate several things, including a visitation or delivery of a message or symbol. Their appearance can certainly have more than one meaning—how do you tell the difference? Many say that there is a visceral element in a visitation that is not present when the person showing up in the dream is there as a symbol or metaphor. My friend Kimberly said that she could feel her mother touch her cheek in her dream. My colleague Fran says that she can sometimes feel the soft weight of her cat sleeping on her chest years after his passing.

Other people who experience visitation dreams from loved ones say that they can feel a sense of being hugged or another expression of love or care. Workshop member Nancy had a dream within a dream. She dreamed her beloved husband Peter was kissing her, and that she then woke up while inside the dream to tell everyone that she had been dreaming of him, and what he said to her. When she actually awoke for real, she wrote in her journal, "I woke feeling so happy, like he had really come to be with me." There is often a felt sense of presence in these dreams. When my dad shows up in my dreams, sometimes I hear his voice with all his familiar tones and timbres.

A consensus exists among dreamers who report visitations, as well as among psychics who channel these types of visits, that a sense of deep connection is felt in a visitation dream. The energetic quality of the beloved visitor is true to the energy of the person who passed. Dreamers often report that very little else happens in the dream besides the visit. That is, there is not a lot of other narrative or story; the visit is the main event.

When I posed the question of how to tell the difference between visit and symbol to my dream circle, they talked about feelings of awe and joy in visitation dreams. These dreams almost always feel like what Jung calls "Big Dreams"—they stand out and are anything but ordinary. Instead, they are momentous or awe-inspiring or comforting. Oftentimes, they are in high-def or technicolor. It's a beautiful metaphor for crossing over from an ordinary experience of life to an extraordinary experience.

Shamanic practice teaches us that sometimes the visitation comes in the dream, and other times it comes in waking life in an animal form, like my cardinal dad. Often no dream interpretation feels necessary with these visitation dreams, except to say, "Hi, I love you, nice to see you again."

For many years after losing her partner in a motorcycle accident, my colleague Melanie dreamed of him. At first she felt his presence as a visit, but now after twenty years she experiences his occasional appearance in her dreams as a symbol. She no longer experiences that vivid sense of his presence, nor does she have a visceral response. She dreams of him much less frequently, and when he does show up, he is not even the CI (central image) any longer. This is a teaching about the trajectory of the purpose of visits. Melanie now feels that she doesn't need his guidance in the same way anymore, so he ceased the actual visits. She is happily married and has a son, and has moved on emotionally in her life.

This Side of the Veil: Our Dream Companions

In his blog mossdreams.blogspot.com, Robert Moss says that in our dreams, "We encounter a whole family of aspects of our-selves, and as we recognize them and bring them together, we become much more than we were." Wordplay is a fun aspect of decoding the symbolism of the people that appear as charac-ters in our dreams. Sometimes the significance is found in their names or in wordplay based on a name, instead of in the presence of a particular person in a dream.

My colleague Mia dreamt of a set of Hartman luggage, which is an actual brand. After some discussion in our dream circle of who "Mr. Hartman" could be, someone noticed that the name could also be heard as "heart man." We then moved into a useful conversation about the man of her heart and how that related to her dream.

Dream wordplay can have layers of meaning. For example, you dream about an Aunt Missy, either an actual person in your life or an imaginary relative. One layer of meaning may be that you are "missing" something, or something is "missing" in your life. Another layer could involve a question about single or mar-ried status (Miss vs. Mrs.).

In dreams that are not visitations, you can classify the dream characters in one or more of the following five categories:

1. **They come as themselves.** Mom really is mom in the dream. The person you know appears in the dreamscape without symbolism.

2. **They come as a symbolic stand-in for someone else.** The woman with the bouffant hairdo who is not my mom in real life is actually my mom in the dream. Stand-in characters sometimes have a symbolic tie-in with the people they represent, so in this case the hairdo tells me who the character represents.

3. **They appear as an archetype.** This Jungian term implies the embodiment of a primordial image or character. Jung believed that these are universal and reside in the collective unconscious (our group mind, if you will) that we share as a species. Archetype examples include the Witch, the Trickster, or the Lover.

4. **They represent a part of yourself.** They may be an aspect of yourself that you need to befriend, heal, reclaim, come to terms with, or simply get to know better, and are depicted in your dream as a separate character. For example, the screaming woman may be an aggressive or a frustrated part of you, the hiding man may be a timid or fearful part of you, or the boss on the job may be a powerful part of yourself. You can use the Gestalt method of dreamwork with these characters and ask yourself, "What is the Jack Smith part of me?" or "What is the long-distance runner part of me?"

5. **They are a guide or a higher being.** They come to give us precognitive information or spiritual direction. He or she may be a commonly known figure like Archangel Michael or Buddha or Persephone (goddess of the underworld). They

may have some numinous sacred quality, but sometimes our guides come disguised as tricksters or unsavory characters or people we have known. The down-and-out street person in our dream can also be our spiritual guide in disguise. There is an old cult classic called *The Kin of Ata Are Waiting for You* that reveals a washerwoman as a spiritual guide.

We already know that dreams can have several layers of simultaneous meaning; so your dad, or your boss, or your friend Julie may be representing more than one thing in your dream. Because we can't see all of our own layers, doing dreamwork with others helps us find what we might not consider without the extra set of eyes and ears.

To explore the five categories, let's use Aunt Missy as the character who showed up in your dream. Here are some questions you can ask to see how many of the five categories she falls into.

1. If she has come as herself, ask yourself who Aunt Missy is to you. Is she from your mother or father's side of the family, and how is that relevant? What is your relationship with her like? Is she your confidant, your second mother, a source of tension on holidays? Do you have any unfinished business with her? What was your last encounter with her like? Do you have a striking memory that includes her?

2. If she has come as a symbolic stand-in, you could ask: What are the qualities or characteristics of Aunt Missy? Is she kind or bossy or pathologically late to every gathering? Do any of these resonate for you about someone else important in your life? What does she look like? Sound like? Does she remind you of anyone? What does she do in the dream?

How do you connect with what she does, such as a task or behavior? Does wordplay with her name resonate with you?

3. If she is an archetype, we might notice: Is she a larger than life figure? Does she remind you of a mythological or fairy tale character or a figure from sacred literature or the tarot? Does she seem to embody one of the primal archetypes, such as the Wise Woman, the Mother, the Witch, or the Shadow?

4. Is there an aspect or part of yourself that you recognize that is like Aunt Missy? Like her, are you … Struggling with a family member? Too passive? High-spirited? The center of your home and family?

5. As a guide or spiritual being: Does Aunt Missy have any numinous or spiritual quality about her in the dream? Does she seem to be glowing? Is she dressed in an unusual way that connects you to something sacred, such as a white dress or long, hooded cape? Does she have a message or guidance for you personally? If Aunt Missy is your guide, what has she come to tell or show you? You may need to engage with her in virtual or actual conversation to find out. Let's now turn to this method of working with your dreams.

The Healing Conversation

In order to engage more fully with your dream characters you can set up an imaginary dialogue with them. One way to do this is to place yourself inside of your dream in your waking imagination, using the technique of dream reentry. See yourself inside the dream setting and landscape encountering your dream character. Then create an imaginary dialogue, articulating both your own voice and that of the dream character, using a Jungian process called active imagination. Imagine the scene and then speak or write down a dialogue in which you pose questions or speak to the dream character, and then listen with your inner ears for the answers and write those down too. Don't worry if it feels awkward, or like you are making it all up; this is a common feeling. Keep going anyways and try to put your analytic brain on hold for now; let your dreaming, creative brain take over both sides of the conversation.

The questions can be quite generic, like "Why are you here?" or "What have you come to tell me?" Or they can be more specific, such as "In my dream you seemed to be warning me of something—could you be more specific about what you meant?" or "I got the sense that you were giving me a gift in the dream, but I couldn't tell what it was; can you clarify that now?" Keep going with your questions and answers until you feel a sense of completion.

You can also dialogue with dream characters from a stance outside of the dream. This is a chance to have an imaginary dialogue in which you tell them what you can't or couldn't say in life, make amends, or apologize, whether this person is still alive or deceased. Write down what you say and ask, and then listen with your heart, your mind, and your body for the response from the other and write that down too so that you are creating a dialogue. Again, don't worry if it feels contrived, or like you are making it up. Ultimately what matters is that you get a sense of resolution on an issue or a complicated relationship. If they are alive, you then have the option of taking this conversation into waking life if you so choose.

If you are dialoguing with a departed loved one with whom you have unfinished business, try entertaining the belief that where they are now they are made of pure spirit and no longer connected with the mistakes or vagrancies of their embodied life. As a spirit, they have transcended any earthly grudges or arguments or misunderstandings, and so are free to reengage with you from that place of pure energy and pure love and forgiveness, even as they retain the recognizable imprint of the person you knew.

Don't forget to notice what the character is doing in the dream, and how you are interacting with him or her. If Grandma is in your dream, what is she doing? Is she cooking, or driving a car, or yelling at you? And what are you doing in the scene with her? Are you the passenger in the car, in the back or the front seat, is anyone else in the car with you? Remember to examine your emotional resonance with her both in the dream and in life. Our emotional associations to the people in our dreams contain the core of the message. The emotion you have inside or about the dream at any given point makes it specific to you, rather than general.

The multiplicity of layers of meaning with the people in your dreams can also be really fun if you dream of famous people. If Madonna shows up in your dream, you can have a field day! Is the dream about sexuality? Or a shadow side of purity? (As in the Virgin Mary from one of her famous songs "Like a Virgin") Or about a different song that you associate with the singer? Or about strong powerful women? Or a judgment of any of these? Or of yourself? Of others? Of a tension between your inner goddess, your sexual self, and your early religious training? A part of you that wants expression? Are you "mad"(-onna) about something? Is there a "Don" in your life? Have fun with it.

Having examined working with our dream characters, animal friends, and relatives, let us now turn to additional methods for understanding the meanings of our dreams.

EXERCISE

Take a character from one of your dreams and work through the five categories of questioning described in this chapter to ascertain the various reasons why they showed up in your nocturnal world (they come as themselves, as a symbolic stand-in, as an archetype, as an aspect of yourself, or as a spiritual guide). Dialogue with the character using active imagination, and even try dialoguing with a group of characters. Allow yourself to generate both sides of the conversation as you "listen in" to what the response from the character might be. Let yourself be surprised by what emerges, and try not to censor any ideas or dialogue until you have fully considered their relevance for your life. Continue the dialogue until you feel a sense of completion.

Remembering that departed loved ones may now be part of a universal energy field, they are therefore not still bound by their embodied life's faults and issues. You now have the freedom to engage with them in ways that you may not have been able to when they were alive, and can now have contact with them from the heart while gaining wisdom, consolation, forgiveness, resolution, or connection with them from the highest parts of each of you. If a departed loved one showed up in your dream, ascertain whether or not it was a simple visitation, or if there is additional meaning or repair that can be done now with this person. Have that healing conversation we spoke of earlier.

Finally, if you had an animal visitor, go over all of your own associations with this animal to see what are relevant, and then use one of the excellent resources from a book or the internet to examine additional numinous or totemic qualities that may apply to your dream animal.

Ten

MAKING MEANING
FROM OUR DREAMS

"Merrily, merrily, merrily, merrily,
life is but a dream."

What does my dream mean? This is what most of us really want to know when we awaken from a strange or scary or delicious dream. Conforti believes that every interpretation of a dream tells us something that our soul already knows. So as we delve into the meanings of our dreams, we are in essence remembering something that we know at a soul level. We recognize this most easily when we have confirmatory dreams, which reassure us that we are on the right path with something. It is also true when we have to dig deeper into the dream to find the meanings in the messages.

Our dreams can feel bizarre—they've been called hallucinations without drugs, and sometimes they are full of everyday things put together in unusual combinations. Either way, our desire to know the meaning of our dreams entices us to find out how to do it—how to "unpack the suitcase," as Jung says—and in this chapter you will find a wide variety of methods and techniques to use in unpacking that dream suitcase.

Existential psychologist and author Erik Craig says, "While dreaming, we entertain a wider range of human possibilities than when awake." Let's tap into this wider range of possibilities to enhance our inner and our outer worlds.

The art of interpreting and understanding a dream is known by a variety of names: dreamwork, dream tending, dream exploration, dream journeying, unpacking the dream. All imply mining the dream for the treasures granted by our emotional, spiritual, physical, mental, and energetic selves. I am particularly fond of the term *unpacking*. I like the metaphor of unpacking a tightly packed suitcase one piece at a time, examining each item until we have emptied our dream suitcase of all the treasures and the "baggage" that was inside. If the suitcase is very tightly packed, we may have to shake out each item well—exploring it using all the tools at our disposal—to get the wrinkles out!

The metaphor of luggage or packing and unpacking reminds me of a therapists' cartoon (my favorite kind; you've gotta be able to laugh at yourself in this biz). An airline counter attendant is presiding over a check-in counter labeled "Emotional Baggage Check-In." He asks the prospective traveler, "Has your baggage been with you at all times?" She replies, "Unfortunately, yes." He then asks, "Has anyone asked you to carry anything?" To which she responds, "You have no idea how many times!" Working with your dreams can help you to lighten your baggage so that you don't have to carry anything extra or something that is not really yours to carry.

My Dream or Yours?

Dreams are very personal. Each one is idiosyncratic to the dreamer and the particular context of their life. We dream in our own lexicon of symbols and images. Each character, landscape, and object in our dreams has personal meaning to us, our own set of associations behind the symbolism, plus a wider potential for meaning drawn from archetypes and collective experience, which may aid others as well as ourselves. An image that means one thing to me in a dream might mean something very different to you. For example, if I dream about a bird it might have something to do with flight or soaring, but for you it might have to do with nesting, or even panic (think Hitchcock's movie *The Birds*). Jeremy Taylor recommends that we preface our ideas about another person's dream with the phrase, "If this were my dream..." in order to honor the personal nature of the dream and not impose our own viewpoint. This respects the dream and the dreamer.

On the other hand, our dreams may have wider resonance than personal symbols, as images based on shared associations from our cultural context and universal symbols from our collective unconscious show up across cultures. We collectively share in this "dream-weave" of thought and spirit, and in this universal symbolism.

This aspect of dreamwork underscores the value of getting others' associations to our dreams, whether our friends' input or an internet search for solid sources of information about dream symbols. When we work in a group, we cast a wide net around the circle to draw in the group's energies and associations, then slowly pull in the ends of the net to see which dream fish we have captured are relevant for our own dream. This is particularly useful with a complex dream.

When dream group member Beth dreamed about bees, we cast a wide net and began to draw in other group member associations of honey, stinging, allergies, the letter B, buzzing, nectar, and bebop. As we drew the net in closer for Beth's own resonances with the bees in her dream, many of our suggestions sifted out through the strands of the net, except for buzzing, stinging, and the old-fashioned phrase "bees in your bonnet." Those resonated with her. By brainstorming associations as a group, we landed in the right ballpark for this particular bee dream. In her dream she deals with the annoying or dangerous kind of bees, not the helpful ones that only want to make honey. Beth had been struggling with a group of very critical and intrusive colleagues on her job, and was feeling "stung" by them.

It's worth repeating that what resonates as true for the dreamer is the most important indicator of the true meaning of their dream. By using embodied dreamwork and attending to not only your thoughts and emotions, but also to your body sensations, you activate your internal Geiger counter. You can discover the "hot zones" in your life by noticing body sensations accompanying the dream, much as a Geiger counter finds sources of radiation. Pay attention to the subtle signs that indicate that you are on the right track, such as a feeling of "bone-knowing," a tingle, a pop, or a shiver of recognition. This uncanny bone-knowing is Gendlin's felt sense, which I spoke of previously. One of his books is entitled *Let Your Body Interpret Your Dreams*. Exactly! A sudden flow of tears or laughter can indicate that you have uncovered a deep truth. I have been known to say, "If I'm crying, it must be right" as I hit an insight I may not have seen before. Breaking into laughter, eyes welling up with tears, letting out a deep spontaneous sigh—these are all signs of a shift in your state of being and a corresponding shift in your knowing what is true for you. These are somatic embodied responses to your dreamwork.

Dreamwork is not a "top-down" expert or a dream dictionary telling you what it true. Rather, the friends, relatives, therapists, or books you consult with should serve as guides asking good questions. Perhaps they also offer options or point out things that they have noticed, but they don't tell you what your own truth is. That's your job. That's "bottom-up."

The Emotional Narrative and the Context of the Dream

The emotions in our dreams are the compass signals that point us to the personal meaning of that dream or image, and connect with our deeper truths, as we learned in chapter 8 on dreams, creativity, and healing. To use this compass, ask yourself, "What was I feeling in this dream overall, in each section of this dream, and after I woke up?" Different emotional reactions to the same image or event imply a very different meaning. For example, are you feeling delighted or mortified to show up naked on a nude beach in this dream? Depending on the emotion connected to this scene there are very different meanings, ranging from sensual or freedom from constraints to feeling overexposed or embarrassed.

The sequencing of the emotional narrative also provides us with a barometer on our progress for resolving an issue. If the dream starts out with us feeling anxious, but by the end we are feeling safe and at peace, then we are probably well on our way to having resolved the dilemma highlighted by the dream. The dream may be a progress report or, as dreamworker Kirsten Backstrom calls it in her blog on compassdreamwork.com, a confirming dream to tell us we are on the right track. Josh, our dreamer from chapter 5 who had the dream of the masked shadow man in the forest, had been working on self-esteem and trying to break a pattern of finding flawed father figures in his boyfriends. He had a confirming dream, wherein he saw his ex, George, at a party, and knew that he was narcissistic, but saw others fawning all over him. He thought to himself in the dream that he didn't have to like George even if the others did, and felt just fine about that as the dream ended.

This is in contrast to his previous dream in which he followed a masked man into a forest. When the man revealed himself by taking off the mask, he was not who Josh thought he was, and had a sinister smile. This time, Josh saw the dream character for exactly who he was, no false masks here. All was revealed and he ended this dream feeling quite proud of himself—a great dream confirmation of being true to his authentic self.

If your dream ends with you feeling distress, however, that points to the need for more healing work on the issues highlighted in the dream, which may be why you had it in the first place. Where and when the events and the emotions occur in a dream, whether at the beginning, the middle, or the end, are important indicators of your current relationship with the dream content. How the dream has ended before you have started to work on it indicates what direction you need to take. In his previous dream, Josh was taken in and duped by the masked man in the end. In the later dream, there was no masking, and in fact, Josh saw who the dream character really was better than anyone else.

Context can refer to one of two things: either what was going on in your life when you had the dream and the relationship of the dream to those life events, or what else is going on inside the dream as you focus on a particular image or part of it. The personal check-ins we have at the beginning of each dream circle serve to provide current background about the life of the dreamers, and this contextualizes the dreams that are then shared.

Whenever we meet, we first have a quick personal check-in before we start the dreamwork. Then, when we do the dreamwork, we almost inevitably find some element within the dream being shared that directly relates to the check-in, even if the circle member is not cognizant of it beforehand. For example, during check-in, one member reported some communication issues with her partner. In the dream she shared later, she had lost power in her home, all the phone lines were down, and her cell phone was uncharged as well. If we step back from the dream, the references to communication issues at home are obvious, but she didn't realize it until someone else pointed out the connection. Those pesky blind spots!

The second meaning of the word context can be the context of the image or event within the dream itself. What is that bird doing in the dream? Is it hiding its head under its wing, flying through the air with a flock of other birds, pecking for worms? This intra-dream context can provide clues to the meaning. As you work with dreams over time, you may develop a lexicon of familiar and common themes that give you a shortcut in the decoding process, your own personal Rosetta Stone.

In the Beginning: How to Start Unpacking Your Dreams

We can work with a dream from the inside out or the outside in. That is, we can describe our dream in the third person—"I had this dream last night where I was walking down the street and …"—or we can enter the dream and speak about it in the first person—"I am walking down the street…" Both are valid ways of working, and as you will see, sometimes we use both styles in the same piece of dreamwork. You are able to get different information about your dream and your life from each style.

Robert Moss, a shamanic dreamworker with several books reflecting his core teachings of active dreamwork, tells us that the talent for dreamwork is a talent for resemblances—what resembles this or reminds us of something else? Since we know that the coded language of dreams uses symbols, we have to figure out what these symbols mean for us, then determine what we need to do with the information we uncover.

Let me walk with you now through unpacking a dream by using a variety of methods. You'll see that with each method we get a certain layer of meaning, and then need to move on to use another method to get further information. After an overview of the dream and the methods used, I'll separate out and clarify how to use the methods so that they stand out more clearly. Then we will examine a few other styles of unpacking a dream, and I will refer you to Appendix III for a comprehensive list of dreamwork tools.

Disclaimer: I don't usually have toilet dreams. Some people do, including one member of my dream group, so when that symbol reemerges for her, we laugh and say, "Oh, here's that toilet again!" I laughed as I recorded the following dream of mine, knowing the responses it was likely to get from the group. I also wondered right away about the significance, since it falls outside my normal dream lexicon. Here's the dream: I have to use the bathroom and the toilet is dirty. I gingerly clean it up as best I can, and use it. It still overflows a bit. My colleague Cheryl is waiting for me.

I titled the dream "Dirty Toilet." At that point I just let the title emerge organically; I didn't know what the dream meant yet.

When I woke up, I wrote down my initial association, which is the first step to interpreting any dream. My colleague Cheryl, whom I hadn't seen in quite a while, had recently participated in a dream workshop I facilitated. At first, that was all I got by reflecting on the dream, since my alarm rang and I had to rush off to start my work day. A few days later I brought it to my dream circle, and they began asking me questions: "Any practical plumbing problems in your home or office?" (No.) As a metaphor: "Any health-related 'plumbing issues'?" (No.) Since my initial association was to my work life, Lisa asked, "Are you feeling overwhelmed or overflowing in any way at work?" This one was a hit for me. "Yes." Here was my first aha. I got that wave feeling in my body. Significantly, Lisa frequently has dreams related to her work and I usually don't, so her resonance with my dream followed her own common associations and led me to my own insight.

My first association to Lisa's question was to the larger than usual number of workshops I was preparing for at the time. I was feeling a bit "overflowing" with all the preparation, but this was only a small aha, so I knew there would be another layer. The next association I had was to doing some dreamwork with a particular client, Paula. Something resonated here too, but I didn't know what yet. I felt that I wasn't making enough headway with this line of questions though, so I moved into another way of working the dream. I now used the Gestalt style, which involves becoming the person or object in the dream and then speaking from that insider perspective.

In order to do this, first I asked myself, "What is the CI, the central image in this dream?" and replied, "the toilet." So I had to speak from the perspective of the toilet. Using the Gestalt method, I asked myself, "If I am the toilet, what do I need?" Speaking as the toilet itself (yes, we do that in dreamwork), the answer that emerged was, "I need to enlarge my bowl, to enlarge the container to be able to hold everything that gets dumped in here without overflowing and making a mess on your shoes."

Now we were getting somewhere—I felt a big aha when I spoke from the perspective of the toilet. I could feel the rightness of that answer in my bones. Becoming the object in my dream allowed me to have a perspective about my work with Paula that I hadn't had before. Another aha emerged, twofold this time: (1) part of my work with Paula was to help her to enlarge her own capacity to be able to hold the pain in her life without it overflowing so much that she couldn't function, and (2) I also needed to enlarge my own sense of presence and my own capacity to hold her pain as I sat with her, in order to safely contain her and her work.

After doing this piece of Gestalt work, I next had a spontaneous association to an old Buddhist teaching tale. This is an example of connecting to the larger archetypical association we referenced earlier. I tried to follow my thoughts and not discount any of them until I had unraveled the thread completely to see if it was relevant to my dream.

Here's the teaching tale I remembered. A woman who had lost her child was in deep despair, and after months of wandering she approached the Buddha and asked for help. "Oh, Enlightened One, I am suffering so much since the loss of my son that I can't bear it. Can you help me?" He replied, "Of course, my dear. But first, you must walk throughout the land and bring me word of at least one being that has not experienced suffering in their life; that is the first step. Now go, and come back to me with that information."

So the woman went and walked for days and weeks and months, and everywhere she went, she found people who had lost a child, or a parent, or their leg, or their crops, or their home— on and on. Finally she returned to the Buddha and said, "Oh, Enlightened One, I have searched and searched, and I cannot find anyone who has not had some suffering in their life." The Buddha responded, "Exactly right. Every being at birth is given

10,000 measures of joy and 10,000 measures of sorrow. The difference between a life of joy and a life of suffering is the size of the container we hold them in."

He went on to offer the woman a cup of water into which he placed a large spoonful of salt. "Taste it," he requested. "It's salty," she replied. Then they went to the lake. The Buddha put the same large spoonful of salt into the lake, then scooped up a cup of the water for the woman to taste. "It tastes sweet and fresh," she said. Same salt, same cup of water. The difference was the size of the original container.

Enlarging the size of the container was the central message of the toilet dream. The associations felt complete. I knew what I needed, and why I had the dream. Now I needed to figure out in practical terms how to manifest them in real time both in my own life, and with that particular client. How could I help Paula enlarge her capacity to contain both the sorrows and the joys in her life, as I do for myself? For starters, in our next session, I told her the story of the Buddha.

Let's now unpack the methods used in this dreamwork.

Unpacking the Multiple Methods

The first thing I did was title the dream, a great way to cut to the chase and quickly tune in to what may be the heart of the matter. I always encourage my dreamer to let the title just emerge from their gut. If it surprises them, so much the better. The title may or may not make sense initially, but don't edit your gut response; it often contains the dark wisdom of your unconscious thoughts emerging into the light of consciousness.

Next, I quickly skimmed for initial associations and only got one from this dream, since I was rushed for time that morning. You may get one, or several, or none. Then I consulted with others, who asked me good questions. You can do this by asking yourself or by having others ask provoking questions. The questions began with the literal (P'shat) level of the dream—are there any real life issues going on that are not symbolic (in this case, plumbing)—and continued from there.

After that we moved to the prodromal or health question: symbolically, did I have any "plumbing" issues in my body that I was aware of, or that the dream might be pointing me toward examining? We then turned to the metaphors embedded in the dream, and other associations based on the word *overflowing*. It is the reverse of the process of casting a wide net and letting things sift out; here, we gradually widen the net as some ideas don't stick and we need to find others. As I tune into my felt sense and embodied responses to the questions, I'm able to follow each thread until I get a hit.

I then used the Gestalt method of becoming the CI in the dream. This can be a lot of fun and provide amazing information that you would not otherwise dream of. By embodying and then giving voice to the toilet, I was able to get perspectives on my work with a particular client that I may not have otherwise considered. A larger world association of a sacred teaching tale came to me then, and even though I didn't get how it was connected at first, I stayed with the story until the relevance of it became clear. Finally, I began the process of creating an action plan based on this dream wisdom, which included both a direction for the therapeutic work and telling my client the Buddha story.

Now let's examine additional items among the smorgasbord of options for dreamwork. Beginning at the end for a minute, it is important to remember that the final stage of dreamwork is the action stage—taking some form of action in our life from the ideas and information we generate. I mention this first so we can orient ourselves in the direction we ultimately want to travel. As we learned earlier, if we first face in the direction of our destination we can utilize the course correction that our dreams provide. The action part of dreamwork is often neglected, which is why some dreams or themes repeat, or some nightmares may continue. The actions we take to honor the dream serve to bring about the life changes we need or desire as well.

Ritual is one of the tools you can use to make an action change in your life. Artist Tania Marie cites psychologist Robert Johnson, who recommends ritual enactment. He believes that "the unconscious can scarcely distinguish between real acts and symbolic ones." You can honor the dream and its teachings by the rituals of saying a prayer, lighting a candle, or burying something symbolic under the tree in your yard. You can have a reminder word or phrase written down on a notecard or used as your screensaver to remind you of what you now know or need to do based on your dream's wisdom. This also is where expressive arts come into play. Doing something may mean creating art, music, dance, or writing based on your dream.

Here are some additional options for dreamwork.

Your Dream, Your Creative License

I often tell the dreamers I work with, "This is your dream, it came from your psyche. Therefore, you have the creative license to go inside and make any changes you'd like, to restructure it, to make a different choice, or to change the ending." Where you thought it ended is not necessarily the end; it is just where you woke up or stopped remembering it! You now have an opportunity to resolve it differently. This is called dream re-scripting or dream re-ending. One of my clients calls it her re-dreaming. Work from inside the dream and add resources, guides, or directives. Dream it forward.

If the dream ended with you on a sinking ship in a roiling sea, add a lifeboat that suddenly appears to save you, or a wizard that waves a hand over the waves and calms the sea, then what happens? Continue the dream story with this new ending. The Talmud tells us that there is a gift in every dream, including in every nightmare. So keep going with your dream, re-scripting until you have received the gift.

Lightning Dreamwork

This five-step formula created by Robert Moss includes some previously mentioned dreamwork methods, ending with the focus and attention on your action plan. It is a quick yet comprehensive formula that may help you to get efficiently to the heart of your dream.

1. *Title your dream:* Doing so can allow the core message of the dream to pop in high relief. Don't overthink it—just go with your first response.

2. *Describe the feeling narrative:* Name the various emotions that accompany each part of the dream story. Walk through the dream and highlight the emotional story that goes with each scene. (I choose sometimes to write the feeling narrative, the storyline of the feelings, alongside the dream content after journaling a dream, to help clarify the connections.)

3. *Bridge to life:* This part is the reality check. Where in waking life might these aspects of the dream be true? Do you recognize the people or places or events in your dream—any of them? Are any of them real people or places that are or were part of your life? You may need to ask several questions here

to tease out possible connections. Once you have the hit or connection, what is the message of the dream for you?

4. *Bumper sticker:* If you were to make a slogan, a pithy statement, or a bumper sticker one-liner out of the main message your dream is bringing to you, what would it be? What does your bumper sticker summation then mean to you?

5. *Action plan to honor the dream:* In order to make a life change or resolve repeating dreams, you need to do something concrete in response. Your action plan may also be to incubate another dream revealing what to do next, or to perform some small symbolic act. The key is to actually DO something.

In a Flash: Lightning Dreamwork

Here we will examine an example of how the lightning dreamwork method worked for my client Carolyn. Her dream falls under the category of what we might call a "bad dream," a sort of a nightmare, so it's a good example to use here as we bridge between this chapter and the next one on working with nightmares.

Carolyn dreamt that she stopped on the way home from work to buy a loaf of bread. When she got home she discovered that it was stale and crawling with bugs. She tried to pick them out, but they were too numerous and it was gross.

Carolyn had been having some version of this dream (sometimes sour milk, sometimes spoiled meat, sometimes at her office, sometimes on the way home) for several months. The dreams were profoundly distressing and didn't dissipate.

Step 1: She titled it "Buggy Bread."

Step 2: The feeling narrative accompanying the dream story was that at first she just felt tired from work; then she started to feel anxious and nervous as she unwrapped the bread; and then when she got it fully unwrapped, she felt disgusted, sickened, and upset.

Step 3: We played with possible bridges to life: Have you bought bread recently? Anything significant about buying bread or having it turn out spoiled in some way when you got it home? How about when you are on the way home from work—how do you usually feel then? Are you feeling sick or disgusted or "bugged" anywhere in your life? Here Carolyn got an aha about some relationship to work.

Then I asked about the significance of bread as a word or symbol. Is it sustenance? Stuff of life? Money? Are you feeling stale or bugged or disgusted at work, the place from which you are to "bring home the bread"? We kept going with the ideas and associations until we hit the mark. Carolyn resonated fully with the references to her work life and felt that was where we'd find the core of the issue.

Step 4: Carolyn explored possible bumper sticker summations of the dream's message, such as these:

"Man does not live by bread alone."
"Call the exterminator."
"Change bakeries."
"Time to go gluten-free."

The bumper sticker she chose read, "Change bakeries," and as she chose it she realized that it might be time to leave her current job. The "bugs" at this workplace were too numerous to continue there. She could risk getting sickened. The bumper sticker then fed the action plan.

Step 5: Carolyn made two action plans. Her small symbolic action plan was to wash her hands before leaving work (to wash the office off) and her second action plan was to start sending out new resumes.

A few weeks later, once she updated her resume and began sending it out, she had another dream. In this one she was baking a cake, and realized in the middle of setting out her supplies that she didn't have all the ingredients. She needed to go to the store, but worried that it was too late and that the store would already be closed, but she went anyway. When she got there it was still open and she could get the rest of what she needed for this cake project.

This was a dream of a different color than the first one. No more bugs; some self-efficacy as she goes out to the store; and it's not too late to get what she needs to complete her project. Although she was not out of the woods yet, the dream was clearly not nightmarish anymore. Carolyn's work on her repetitive dreams and choosing her action plans based on the new dream-based knowledge enabled her to change the old internal pattern generating her repetitive upsetting dreams, and a few months later a new job appeared on her horizon.

Change your dream, change your life. Now let's take this information with us as we move into the most distressing yet important part of dreamwork: dealing with and healing from nightmares.

EXERCISE

See Appendix III for an extensive summary of dream-work methods. Then choose a medium-sized dream from your recent dream life to unpack. I suggest medium-sized to start with so that you have both sufficient dream content to try out many methods, but not such a big one that you become overwhelmed with too many details. If a long dream is calling to you loudly, perhaps choose a section of it to focus on, or find the CI and work with the material connected to just that image.

Read over the appendix and decide which methods your dream is seeking—you can use both your cognitive responses and your felt sense to ascertain the methods you want to use. You can also try the short lightning dream process to get quick hits. Whatever methods you use, be sure to write down your insights and observations on the same page as your dream, so that you can easily cross reference between the dream content and your associations, connections, and plans for resolution and action. Remember to also record your emotions and somatic sensations, as they will be important indicators of both the meaning of your dream and your progress working on it. Finally, once you have gotten as much juice and information out of the dream as you need or want right now, don't forget to formulate and put into action a physical plan or manifestation of your desired goal. It can be a small symbolic gesture implied by the dream or the dreamwork, something in writing, or a physical action or movement. Do something concrete in the waking world to honor your dream insights; this will make the manifestation of them much more alive and generate their potential.

Eleven

TAMING DEMONS AND
TRANSFORMING NIGHTMARES

"Dreaming is a healing process ... a vital
means by which we bind up our wounded
spirits and rekindle our hopes for the future."
Kelly Bulkeley

Nightmares. We've all had some taste of them, from a single mild disturbance to all-out terror and repetitive nocturnal horror shows. Fire is the worst nightmare of our Scarecrow, his deepest fear. So this is what the Wicked Witch threatens him with during the penultimate scene in her castle. She holds her lit broomstick toward him and sets his arm on fire.

Dorothy saves both him and the day by flinging the bucket of water over him and dousing the witch in the process, who then melts away to nothingness. Nightmare thus resolved for Scarecrow, and Dorothy is able to get that broomstick and return to the Wizard. It's not always this simple, but it is a great metaphor for dissolving the things that haunt our dreams and our lives.

In this chapter, we sharpen our focus on what Zorba called the "full catastrophe," in this case referring to the ubiquitous phenomenon of nightmares that weave in and out of our more pleasant dreams. Zorba the Greek, one of my favorite characters, tells us about the full catastrophe, or full range of joy and hardship that is his life, although most of us may be more familiar with this term via Jon Kabat-Zinn and his book *Full Catastrophe Living*. We dread having this sort of dream. But these heart-pounding anxiety dreams can serve to help us to unravel and ultimately heal the issues that plague us most. In her book *Thirst*, Mary Oliver wrote, "Someone I loved once gave me a box full of darkness. It took me years to understand that this, too, was a gift." This wisdom of darkness was revealed to her in a dream as part of a poem entitled "The Uses of Sorrow."

Root Sources of Nightmares

A wide range of phenomena can influence your dreams as well as contribute to nightmares. Yes, that spicy vindaloo you ate last night can be a factor. Certain medications or withdrawal from substances can also cause nightmares; these nightmares are biologically based. Hormonal changes, such as those due to pregnancy or puberty, can also play a part.

However, the main culprits that generate nightmares are upsetting events you've experienced over the recent days or weeks, unpleasant emotional states you feel stuck in, or earlier traumatic and unresolved parts of your life. The scariest nightmares are frequently a distorted funhouse mirror reflection of

Alchemy Arts, Inc.

1203 W. Bryn Mawr Ave.
Chicago, IL 60660
(773) 769-4970
www.alchemy-arts.com

Monday -Saturday: 10-8
Sunday: 11-6

Cust: **None**

14-Nov-20 4:16p	Clerk: Admin
Trns. #: 20088519	Reg: 1

9780738761824	*Modern Dreamwork*
1 @ $16.99	$16.99

	Sub-total:	$16.99
	Tax @ 10.250%:	$1.74

	Total:	**$18.73**

* Non-Tax Items

Items: 1   Units: 1

Payment Via:

VISA/MC/Discover $18.73

VISA ************1240
Approval: 001617
TroutD: 0043

Sales on Perishable Items are Final - Other
items, whole and unspoiled, may be exchanged
for store credit within 14 days with receipt.
BLESSINGS!

some kind of severe upset or trauma. The repetitive ones usually stem from long-term "unfinished business" from your past, and traumatic events that have not yet been resolved.

Robin, a soft-spoken health care professional, said that her husband tells her that she frequently yells out loud in her sleep, including yelling *"F**k you!"* to unseen dream characters. This has been going on for years, and most recently she had the following dream. Robin dreamt that she was with a close childhood friend, but in the house of another woman, Alice, who had wronged and betrayed her a few years ago as an adult. In the dream, Alice was chasing her. She turned and yelled at her, "F**k you, I'll kill you!"

Robin's outburst was way out of character for anything she'd dream of doing in real life. She woke shaking with fear and rage. Alice really did betray Robin a few years prior to the dream— a waking world connection—but Robin would never have yelled or swore at her. As we worked with the recurring theme of yelling out loud in this dream, Robin told us that the first emotion she felt was fear, and then the anger came afterward. In answering our dream questions, she discovered that, ironically, her fear was that if she actually did get rid of this Alice in her dream (she had already cut ties in her life) then she would then be all alone. This insight brought her to an even deeper fear, a fear within a fear.

The presence of her childhood friend in the dream helped to place the emotional timeframe of the dream in her childhood. This generated an association about her own mother, who suffered from severe depression and "left her all alone" as a teen. We know that family members of those who suffer from various forms of mental illness often have complicated long-term reactions, including rage and a sense of betrayal, along with the loss and grief. Robin had never felt permission to name the anger she felt toward her mother, as that would have been thought of as unseemly.

Examining the dream helped Robin name this anger and betrayal that was a part of her original loss, feelings that were still present many years later in her adult life. This theme had been showing up off and on for years as a series of angry nightmares. As neuropsychologist Daniel Siegel says, we "name it to tame it." Once named, we could work on resolution.

Nightmares can contain visceral physical or sensory memories that have not yet been encoded by our brains into language. When we wake with panic and a pounding heart, but are safe in our beds in our rooms, what is that? The amygdala, a part of the limbic system in our brain, is known as our "emotional accelerator" and is where our fight or flight reactions take place. It can shunt unprocessed raw material to us at night before it has had a chance to be filtered through our thinking prefrontal cortex, where the language centers of our brain are contained.

Repetitive nightmares are an SOS from our unconscious. Our dreaming brain will continue to offer up these fears and perhaps even escalate them to get us to sit up and take notice. The nightmares can cast their shadows on our waking lives as well, generating fatigue, irritability, difficulty concentrating, or a lingering emotional hangover from the dream that lasts throughout the day. Deep and careful work on these unwelcome visits can generate hidden gifts. By using many of the dreamwork tools we learned in chapter 10, as well as the others we will examine here, we can ultimately transform nightmares and free ourselves from their bondage.

Children and Nightmares

In an animated web video, Blank on Blank interviewed author Stephen King, who reminds us that "we think in a different way as children. [As children] we tend to think around corners instead of in straight lines. Sometimes for a kid the shortest distance between two points isn't a straight line. That's the way that we think in dreams."

Children's dreams are affected by upsetting events in their lives, but it is also important to know that having nightmares is a normal developmental stage for many children and not necessarily a sign that something is seriously wrong. From about age three or four until around age eight or nine, children are just beginning to recognize that their previously infallible and all-protecting parents are not perfect, and that the world can be a scary place. This can come as a shock—"What do you mean that you can't make my hamster Joey come alive again?" So now, not only does Tommy have the trauma of his hamster dying, he also has the trauma of his parents being unable to fix it.

It seems that this dawning consciousness for children of this age group—that their parents cannot protect them from everything, as well as the fact that they have to leave the nest for increasing periods of time to begin school and other outside activities—makes this age span a common time for nightmares to occur. Children have to figure out how to negotiate their expanding world, and the anxieties associated with this developmental step can seep into sleep.

For many kids, the nightmares resolve by themselves, with just a little TLC and good parenting techniques. For others, some of the following tried and true methods may help restore them to feeling more competence and agency in their world. Here are a few techniques that are helpful for kids to gain some power over their night monsters (P.S. they work great for adults too).

Vanquishing the Nightmare

1. Never underestimate the power of a good nightlight to chase away the scary darkness.

2. In addition to an actual nightlight, some kids love to have a "monster vaporizer" in the form of a flashlight, which when pointed into all the dark corners and under the bed, will automatically vaporize any lurking dangers.

3. Have them tell the story of the dream out loud, and join them in deciding which objects, other people, or magical/ spiritual beings they want to bring with them into the dream or into the room to keep them safe.

4. Draw a picture of the nightmare, and then change the picture by making it humorous (i.e., put a funny hat on the monster), or adding the magical safety items from #3 to the picture.

5. Once it is safely contained (i.e., put in jail, or in a cage, or behind a fence or a force field), try talking back to the dream monster. Even saying, "Na-na-na-na-na, you can't get me!" or "Go away" can be very powerful for a certain age group.

6. When my daughter was young her personal favorite approach was to draw the dream monster or bad guy and then scribble over it with a heavy black magic marker until it was completely obliterated. Then, if that was not yet enough, rip the paper into tiny shreds. Then, if that was not

yet enough, burn the shreds of paper safely in a big pot or container. Then, if that was not yet enough, flush the ashes down the toilet! (Parts of this method are adapted from a process known as Gentle Reprocessing, developed by Diane Spindler as a variation on the body/mind healing method EMDR.) Keep going with the process until your child gets to a centered and quieted place.

7. Have an actual conversation with the dream monster or bad guy once it is safe to do so. Find out why it is there, what it wants, and how to appease or befriend it. Feed it a cookie. See what gift it has brought for the young dreamer. A great book you can read to young readers and older ones can read to themselves is *A Wizard of Earthsea*, the first book of the EarthSea Trilogy by Ursula K. Le Guin. This magical allegory concludes with the young wizard Ged learning how to face his monsters.

8. Native American dream catchers can be hung over the bed to "catch" the bad dreams, while the hole in the middle lets the good ones come through.

9. And, of course, utilize hugs, lullabies, and cuddling, and the power of your true and loving presence.

10. For those who like acronyms, this is a useful one to help kids with nightmares:

   Describe the dream.

   Reflective listening: "It looks like you're really scared."

   Express reassurance. Not that it is "just a dream," rather that they have your support, that scary

dreams are a common occurrence and you understand how real they feel, and that you will help to
resolve it.

Allies and action: Gather up real and imaginary
resources and take action.

Move and modify: Create movement in the dream
so the child is no longer stuck in the scene, and/
or make modifications to the dream in the middle or the end to resolve the threat.

Seek Safety: Find the long-term solutions as needed;
the goal for the dream and for life is to experience
safety.

Nightmares and Adults

Adult nightmares fall into two categories: the uncomfortable or
upsetting dream, and the heart-pounding, panic-stricken, terrifying one. As Mike Carey writes in *The Naming of the Beasts*,
"Those heart-hammering nightmares that start to lose coherence
even as you're waking up from them, but that still manage to
leave their moldering fingerprints all across your day."

Some nightmares are so vivid that we have physical reactions
to them—we wake sweating or gasping, or, as with Robin, our
partner wakes us up asking, "What were you yelling about in
your sleep?" To truly achieve freedom from the nightmares, we
need to resolve what is generating them.

Facing our fears is part of our life's journey. In Joseph Campbell's *hero's journey*, every hero and heroine encounters obstacles on their journey. They may be confronted with seemingly
impossible tasks that they have to figure out how to resolve and

overcome. Sometimes the task of both the mythic figures and us is to learn some way to face a monster and overcome it. In the myth of Perseus and Medusa, our hero Perseus has to cut off the Gorgon Medusa's head. However, since looking at her snakey head directly would turn him to stone, he has to figure out how to look at her indirectly by using his shield as a reflector, and thus become able to slay her. In this myth, "facing her" means using a reflective shield as a mirror rather than look at her straight on.

Sometimes the hero's task is to journey to dark, forbidding places for the purpose of redemption. In the myth of Orpheus and Eurydice, the hero Orpheus journeys to hell and back to reclaim his bride. Our Dorothy is given all three of these tasks: to face up to her fear of actually meeting the Wizard in order to make her request to go home; to achieve the seemingly impossible task of bringing back the witch's broomstick; and to go into the dark forbidding witch's castle, where she ultimately finds redemption for her own quest and frees the witch's slaves in the process.

Since we know that the language of dreams is usually built of symbols, we have to uncover what our nightmare scenes are telling us, and discover what we need to do with that information. As we learned previously, the final stage of dreamwork is the action stage—taking the wisdom the dream has yielded to create some form of action in our life. This is the part of the dreamwork process that is often neglected, which is why the nightmares may continue. We can transform our nightmares into a resource when we uncover their meanings, take the needed actions, and integrate their messages into our lives. Sometimes that may mean embracing the paradox of befriending our dream monsters, once we have seen that they are actually trying to inform or gift us and not necessarily harm us.

Nightmares as Signs of Healing: Not an Oxymoron

Our dreams show us our internal demons, and at the same time can become sources of healing and solace. This paradoxical alchemy creates meaning out of chaos, hope out of despair, and a forward-moving life force out of the depths of darkness and sorrow. In the *Journal of Clinical Psychology and Psychotherapy*, Diana Fosha writes, "We are all wired for growth. We all have the capacity to feel joy and delight, and nothing that feels bad is ever the last step." These precepts are part of a relationship-centered therapy Fosha developed called AEDP (Accelerated Experiential Dynamic Psychotherapy).

Although hard to believe when they are occurring, post-traumatic nightmares, those nightmares that occur as a result of traumatic experiences, can actually be a sign that a vital life force is pushing forward in an attempt to bring in the potential allies of deep inner strength and resilience. These resources, however, need to be activated and brought forward into consciousness. Dreaming in and of itself is a healing process; one function of dreams is to digest and process information. In response to post-traumatic dreams, I coined the expression, "If we don't metabolize what has happened, we might metastasize it." Whether literal or not, if we don't digest something well, it can repeat on us. Dreamworker Jeremy Taylor reminds us that there is no such thing as a "bad" dream, only dreams that sometimes take a negative form to grab our attention.

However, dreams that follow a crisis do not aim to simply return the dreamer to the status quo. Rather, as Kelley Bulkeley tells us in *Dreams of Healing: Transforming Nightmares into Visions of Hope*, they aim to develop a whole new understanding of the self and the world that encompasses the trauma, and help the dreamer to rise out of the ashes of their broken self "to find new hope, structure, and meaning for their world." Dreams are one of our most powerful sources of meaning making, and following unbearable trauma we will need a new way of making meaning out of our world and our life.

Our dreaming selves are struggling to deal with the psychological distress and spiritual anguish caused by traumatic events. Reflecting on the principle that nightmares can contain within themselves a source or direction for healing, Bulkeley continues, "Nightmares are more like a vaccine than a poison ... Although dream-sharing by itself does not cure a disease, it does have the power to enhance our conscious awareness of both our deepest fears and our greatest strengths."

Nightmares come to us bearing gifts—even the really scary ones. We may not have been particularly desirous of this kind of gift, and would just as soon re-gift it whenever possible. However, if we've dreamed the dream, it means that some part of us is ready to receive gifts of information, insight, potential, or direction that we need to move forward in our lives. Somatic practitioner Peter Levine tells us that trauma once resolved is a force that enhances and enriches our lives.

EXERCISE

We can assist our dreaming selves in this healing process whether our nightmares stem from trauma, loss, illness, or parts unknown. Try incubating dreams of healing and resolution at night before going to sleep. Spend a few moments quietly tuning in, and then write in your dream journal about your desire for your dream guides to send you healing dreams—in the service of your highest good and best interests. You can be general or specific, depending on what you already know about your nightmares or distress. We can orient ourselves, as the Talmud suggests, to finding the gift in every dream. If you receive another nightmare, check to see if there is some redemptive aspect in it that may not have appeared in your previous nightmare as a result of your focused attention on bringing in healing before going to sleep.

Working through Repetitive Nightmares

When we recognize the patterns in our dreams and in our lives, we then have the power to shift and transform them.

Amanda, age eight, developed a fear of intruders breaking into her house following the Boston Marathon bombing. Her town had been put on lockdown while the police were searching for the perpetrators. She dreamed over and over that someone would break in and kidnap or hurt her or her family members and pets.

Jen, age twenty-seven, consistently dreamed of violence—being chased by a giant, someone being murdered, small animals being hurt. Her current life was pretty stable and happy, so she couldn't figure out what these dreams were about.

What both of these dreamers have in common is the repetitive and intrusive nature of their dreams. Sometimes bad dreams and nightmares resolve on their own, and sometimes they seem to get stuck on replay. Tracking the repetitive dreams is crucial for finding and healing the patterns. We probably won't recognize the patterns if we don't keep track of them and record them over time. Only with attention will the patterns emerge.

Healing starts with becoming aware of the patterns that sabotage our lives. Once aware, we can begin to heal them. Sometimes we already know the events that happened in our life that are generating the nightmares; sometimes we need to sleuth them out. Other times we can simply work inside the dreams themselves to make changes that resolve the nightmare without knowing for sure what the source is.

Alan Siegel, past president of the International Association for the Study of Dreams (IASD) outlines three stages in the resolution of recurring nightmares: the threat, the struggle, and the resolution. In the initial dream or dreams, the threat is apparent, such as "I am chased by a bear." Then, most likely in a later dream, the story evolves, some kind of struggle takes place, and the main character makes a little progress. "I climb a tree to get away from the bear, but it lurks at the base and traps me." Finally the dreams generate a solution. "The bear tires and goes away, and I safely climb down and escape into the forest."

I like this organization because it honors the steps along the road to resolution. Looking at it in this way, we can see that even though the middle phase—the struggle—is still difficult, it does represent progress. It's important for us to recognize the small steps along the healing path, as well as the big leaps.

Siegel also provides us with an easy-to-remember outline for the work of healing from nightmares. Many of these steps will sound familiar from the previous chapter on methodology. The "3 Rs" of our childhood were reading, writing, and 'rithmatic. The "4 Rs" of dream healing are reassurance, re-scripting, rehearsal, and resolution.

> *Reassurance:* As dreamworkers, whether we are talking to children, loved ones, or clients, the first step in providing

some comfort and relief to nightmare sufferers is reassur-ance. Not the kind of reassurance that professes "it's just a dream," since that would negate their experience, but reas-surance that you respect the feelings of the dream and you recognize that it feels very real. This reassurance is what Dor-othy wanted from her Auntie Em at the end of the story— "Oh no, Auntie Em. This was a really truly live place." Having a dream be taken seriously is a comfort for both children and adults. Then, helping the dreamer lean into the dream with better resources, rather than leaning away from it in avoidance or fear is a good next step.

Re-scripting: This process allows you to rewrite the nightmare to build in resources for the dreamer to use while working with it, so you can end the dream on a more positive note. We encourage the dreamer to approach scary dreams slowly and carefully, and to add resources for safety and protection even before working with the dream material itself. For example, use your imagination to provide mag-ical tools; cultural symbols or icons; protection items like shields, light, or force fields; or a posse of people/animals/ guides to protect the dreamer. Anne Wiseman, author of *Nightmare Help*, suggests that we avoid using violent means as protection, as this can encourage using violent means to solve life problems, especially with children. Even with adults, we don't want to too quickly annihi-late a dream figure that we may later discover is a hidden resource for us.

Rehearsal: Do you remember the old joke, "How do you get to Carnegie Hall? Practice, practice, practice!" That's what rehearsal is all about: practice using the methods you came up with while re-scripting. Work out and rehearse a safer and more satisfying dream scenario and dream ending. Keep going over those resources, changing the dream ending, getting the characters to talk to each other, and so on until the dreamer can "do it in their sleep."

When working with eight-year-old Amanda, who had the repetitive nightmares of intruders after the Boston Marathon bombing, I helped her practice standing up big and tall and building a magic fence around her house. As we acted that out, she also talked back to the intruders out loud, saying, "Go away, you can't get me!"; "Get out of here!"; and "I'm safe." In Amanda's case, the perpetrators had already been killed or caught by the time she started having these dreams, so we also added that bit of reality for her to rehearse at night before going to sleep as well—"The bad guys are already locked up far away from here."

Resolution: Once we've reassured, re-scripted, and rehearsed, we are much more likely to come to a good resolution. Either the nightmares will disappear, or they will transform into something neutral, benign, or even helpful, and may already provide some insight or direction for the dreamer to take in their waking life. For Jen, once she was equipped with force fields, guardian angels, and Aslan, the lion from Narnia, by her side, she stopped running from the giant who was chasing her in her dream, turned to face him, and asked, "What do you want from me?" To her surprise, the giant replied, "I have been trying to give you this box of big love." That had been one of her mother's pet phrases to her—"big love." It took a big giant to give her back the gift of big love that she thought was gone when her mother died.

PTSD Dreams and the GAIA Method for Healing

Nightmares following significant trauma need a special set of protocols. The first steps in resolving post-traumatic nightmares are containment and safety, followed by reworking and integration of the traumatic experience, and ultimately transformation of the resolved dream into a resource for the dreamer. This protocol mirrors the stages of healing from trauma outlined by Dr. Judith Herman in her classic book *Trauma and Recovery*. It may be important to get professional assistance when working with post-trauma dreams, as these dreams can have long tentacles reaching into the lives of the dreamers.

Some nightmares come packaged with a warning, "Don't try this at home!" Our first mandate as dreamworkers, as for physicians, is "Do no harm." You can use the following GAIA method carefully and share it with professionals trained in trauma treatment for use within a therapeutic setting. If you know that you or the dreamer you are guiding has trauma in their background, and suspect that the dreams may be opening a window into that arena, it may be wisest to stick with providing resources to aid the dreamer in feeling protected. Encourage them to seek professional help for the deeper work. The end of this section will provide you with an example of some clinical dreamwork using this method.

Our psyche does have a capacity for self-healing. Following a trauma, it's common to have a progression of post-trauma dreams that begin with fear, violence, and scenes directly connected to or reminiscent of the traumatic events. This is our psyche processing the upset as we sleep. Dr. Ernest Hartman postulates that the initial dreams following trauma have to do with the fear, terror, vulnerability, helplessness, guilt, and grief we may have experienced. Over a period of weeks or months, as the trauma gradually resolves, the dreams often follow a discernable pattern. There may first be a replay of the event itself over and over. The trauma is replayed vividly and dramatically, but not necessarily in precisely the way it occurred: the dreams can include elements that did not actually happen in life. The content and the emotions then begin to fade on their own if the dreamer is metabolizing the experience.

The emotional resonance guides the dream or nightmare, not necessarily the event itself. For example, we may have survived a car accident, but our dreams throw us images of train crashes, roller coaster mishaps, colliding into a tree while skiing, or other experiences of being out of control. If we are healing from our traumatic experiences spontaneously, we will begin to see a natural progression of our dreams having less intense emotions, vaguer and more fleeting images, and eventually a lack of upsetting images altogether. If the nightmares continue or escalate, it's a sign for more healing work to be done, perhaps with professional help.

Chronic recurring nightmares are often caused by unresolved traumatic events in our lives. These might be personal "Big T" traumas such as a history of neglect or abuse, exposure to violence, substance abuse, medical trauma, or abandonment, which all occur in a private setting. They can also be public traumas, such as a life disrupted by a natural disaster or refugee experiences.

However, even "small t" traumas such as fender benders can spark nightmares. While upsetting in their own right, they can also serve to reactivate some earlier larger-scale trauma. Once the underlying issues have been resolved sufficiently, these night-mares begin to lessen their grip and often disappear entirely. This desired result can be brought about after dreamwork sessions—in some cases just one or two, and in others, many sessions, depend-ing on the precipitating events.

One of my clients, Eva, had nightmares "contaminate" her bedroom so much that she no longer felt able to sleep in her bed. At Christmastime she discovered that the lights on the Christ-mas tree were soothing and comforting for her, and she took to sleeping under it in the living room. She kept renegotiating with her roommates to leave the tree up until April, when they finally declared a hard stop because of the amount of dry pine needles they kept stepping on throughout the house. We fig-ured out together in her therapy sessions that she could buy a small artificial tree to put in her bedroom, strung with colored lights, as a stopgap measure until the nightmares were sufficiently resolved. This was actually a significant step in her healing work. Seeing that she could have greater control over her dream life, and that she could effect change there, she began to generalize that self-agency to other parts of her life as well.

An important note about symbolism in PTSD dreams: When working with nightmares that contain real life events, figures, or actions, we don't know for sure what is symbolic and what is an actual memory emerging in dream form. While dreams gen-erally come encoded in symbolism, sometimes memory bursts of actual events may make their way into the dream world and emerge full-blown. A process known as dissociation may have stored the memory of an actual event in the unconscious to wait for the dreamer to be ready to address it, and it can then burst through the unconscious mind into consciousness in the dream state. Dissociation is a psychological phenomenon that creates memory storage in a part of the brain not usually used for that purpose, and allows us to be "in two places at once," especially during times of extreme trauma. Dissociation is a common mentalization process that can range from "normative dissociation" such as spacing out in class and "highway hypnosis," to shutting down feelings and obscuring memory, all the way to the extreme end of the dissociation spectrum, dissociative identity disorder—what used to be known as multiple personality disorder. The psyche wants to protect itself, and sometimes the only way it can find to do so is to not only wall off chunks of memory, but to actually separate itself out into different personalities in extreme cases of abuse.

When working with the content of traumatic dreams, we should carefully remain neutral about the events until the truth is sussed out, even as we confirm and acknowledge the feelings the dreams create.

The crucial first step in working with very upsetting nightmares is to make sure that the dreamer has enough safety to work on the dream material without becoming re-traumatized in the process. Following years of treating trauma clients and training in many modalities for the treatment of trauma, as well as years of dreamwork, I developed a system of healing from nightmares called the GAIA Method, or Guided Active Imagination Approach. It is based on a combination of Jung's active imagination work and basic safety protocols from the trauma treatment world. Active imagination allows us to engage with dream figures in waking life to provide a bridge between the conscious and the unconscious. It uses the imagination as a tool of transformation. Jung used it primarily to engage with the people in his dreams. I expanded this concept to engage with people, objects, and places, first from outside of the dream to enhance safety, and after that, within the world of the nightmare itself. Having worked with a number of clients who experienced an abreaction (an emotional overload resulting in dysregulation) when doing dreamwork with others without proper care or precautions, I wanted to reduce the possibility of any re-traumatization as much as possible.

The first priority is to make sure that the dreamer has all the resources they need in the waking imaginal realm before they even begin work on the dream content itself. Therefore, the GAIA method progresses in two stages. Stage 1 begins before working on the dream itself, and Stage 2 follows by gathering up the resources developed outside the dream in Stage 1 to be used inside the dream. I'll begin by describing the protocol, and then share an example of how you might use it. Appendix III provides an overview of the method step-by-step.

> *GAIA Method Stage 1:* Ask the dreamer what resources they need to feel safe enough to approach the dream, to be able to reenter it and work on it. So, from outside the dream, after they have shared it, but before going inside to work on it, we first use active imagination to gather up people, objects, guides, and resources that the person can later bring with them into the dreamscape for protection. I can't emphasize strongly enough how important this step is. It can be the difference between gaining healing around the nightmare or getting re-traumatized when working on it. We don't want to barge into hell without adequate preparation and protection. Some of the beings and objects that my dreamers have gathered before entering the dream include a flashlight (it can be dark in there), a baseball bat, an invisibility cloak, their guardian angel, a beloved pet, a friend or relative (both alive and deceased),

and a mythological figure. One client brought Gandalf, the wizard from the Lord of the Rings series. Another client channeled Xena, the Warrior Princess, and some kind of Divine Light. The possibilities are limitless. I continue to ask the dreamer, "Anything or anyone else?" until they say, "All set."

GAIA Method Stage 2: After making sure that the dreamer is safe and ready, we enter the dreamscape using the dream reentry techniques from chapter 10. Then, along with the protection gathered in Stage 1, we use a variety of methods detailed in chapter 10 and appendix III, to work with the dream material from inside the dream. We may engage in a dialogue with a dark character. We may rearrange the dream landscape. We may send Divine Light onto the dream scene to transform it. We may zap the evil one out to the far reaches of the universe.

Toward the end of this process we may include "outcome rehearsal." Here, the dreamer imagines a more positive outcome for the dream, adding in whatever additional resources they need to bring it about, and then they rescript the dream ending. We rehearse this new ending several times until it feels strong and viable. It is important to go slowly and carefully, and not rush to complete the dreamwork if the dreamer feels unsafe at any point. It is better to close down the work on the dream and re-ground with safety and containment, then wait to return at a later date, rather than rush through it too quickly and risk re-traumatizing the dreamer.

Here is an example of using the GAIA method with Nancy's dreamwork story. First, some background on her life. While growing up, Nancy endured years of being sexually assaulted by her father. As an adult, she suffered from nightmares that were so powerful that they affected her all day. She told me that off and on throughout her day she would spontaneously have feelings of dread and the same sensations of claustrophobia and feeling trapped that she had in her dreams. Often her father or mother or her childhood house would feature centrally in her dreams. Although she was now an adult and her father was deceased, the fear generated from her dreams and her trauma history was so strong that she felt the need to binge eat or drink to excess to soothe herself. She despaired of ever being free of her fear.

We started to address her nightmares using the GAIA method. In Stage 1, before working directly on the dreams, she added the resources of her two pet cats, the special blue comforter on her current adult bed, a good friend from her spiritual community, and me standing by her. In Stage 2 of the work, using active imagination inside the dream itself, she gathered up all these resources, then reentered the dream, approached her childhood home, and saw her father there. When asked what she wanted to do next, she replied, "Take away his power over me." To do that, she first surrounded herself with a boundary of white light and tuned in to the support of all the resources she had prepared. She spoke back to him in the dream in a way she had not been able to do as a child, saying to the dream father, "You are dead now. You have no power over me here. I have survived." As she spoke and watched, his image began to fade and become but a pale ghost of his former self.

After several weeks of doing this type of dreamwork, she came in and said, "Linda, I am almost afraid to mention this in case I jinx it, but for the past two weeks, even though I am remembering my dreams, they disappear within minutes of my waking up and they don't bother me during the day." For the next month, she would report every week: "Still no dream hangover—can that be true?" Then one week she came in and said, "When I have dreams of my father now, instead of him being larger than life and menacing to me, he seems little and weak and I am more powerful than him."

These transformations are hallmarks of resolving trauma. The previous active suffering and emotional triggering is transformed into "just a memory" with no emotional wallop. The survivor feels empowered and the abuser's power is diminished or removed. One of Nancy's final dreams in the series involved having her father shrink down to the size of a mouse. She then snared him in a mousetrap, and one of her spiritual guides removed it from the home and disposed of it.

When we are able to lean into our pain and nightmares, rather than run from and block them, we gain access to healing and comfort. It's not always an easy task, or one for the faint of heart. Gathering up our courage along with our resources can lead us home to the sanctuary inside of our own hearts and minds.

EXERCISE

Review your recent or historical but memorable dreams and decide if they fall into the nightmare category. Try working through the dreams using any of the methods described in this chapter, making sure to check in with yourself (or your child if you are helping them) and be sure that you are feeling safe and protected as you do this work. Err on the side of caution if you are unsure, and end the dreamwork with a scene or tools for safety and protection. Consult Appendix

III and follow the steps carefully. You might try the four Rs of reassurance, re-scripting, rehearsal, and resolution with your dream. You might try drawing the scary dream figure and then obliterating it with black magic marker or burning it, or perhaps you want to put it in a cage or behind a force field and have a conversation with it to see what gifts it may have for you. If you are unable to stay grounded in a safety zone, or if you know that there is a trauma history behind the nightmares, please contact a mental health professional with experience in trauma treatment, and ideally in dreamwork as well, to guide and support you through this journey.

Twelve

USING THE WISDOM OF YOUR
DREAMS TO CHANGE YOUR LIFE

"There is much to be learned on both
sides of the threshold."
Christian McEwen

We have traveled this path of dreams together, you and I, over these moonlit and darkening roads. Our world needs strong dreamers today more than ever. As Dorothy found companions to help her on her journey home, we need women and men who can tune in to their own minds and hearts in order to lead us with wisdom, compassion, and leonine courage out of the dark places we keep stumbling into as we journey through life.

We can continue to tread this path to build a community of deep dreamers to heal ourselves and the world around us. When we listen deeply with our bodies as well as with our ears to the whisperings of our souls and the night murmurings of the dreamtime, we can also tune in to this land through our waking glimpses of synchronicity if we are aware of our dreams in the dayscape as well. As we resolve our own dilemmas and heal our own lives, we have more energy available to extend that wisdom and healing out to the world at large.

Jewish tradition teaches us that we are all tasked with *tikkun olam,* "repairing the world." Dreamwork is a powerful tool for repairing both our inner and outer worlds. Just as the final stage of dreamwork is the action we take as a result of understanding what the dream is tasking us with, *showing up* is the beginning of making a difference in our world as well. To build a community of dreamers, we start by showing up.

We can elevate the importance of dreamwork as a viable means of knowledge of self and others, and as an easily accessible GPS for repairing the world. The wisdom traditions of our elders knew this truth. If we take on the commitment of valuing our own dreams, and of honoring them by tracking them, recording them, and thinking about the messages they're trying to reveal, we can rediscover this ancient wisdom of our souls. At the most basic level, we can carry forward our intention to remember and work with our dreams. Here are some ideas for how you can share your dream knowledge with others.

The Power of Dream-Sharing

As we have learned, others may be able to see something in our dreams that we ourselves cannot. We may even feel *sure* that what they see is incorrect. Working in a dream group or with a therapist who is versed in dreamwork can help us to see past our own blind spots. Dream-sharing can allow us to see the back of our own heads, with one or several other dreamers acting as that mirror reflecting perspectives we cannot see on our own. Even Jung himself is famous for saying that he needed to consult with someone to get the full meaning out of his dreams.

The Diamond Method, a psycho-spiritual approach to life, articulated by spiritual teacher and depth psychologist A. H. Almaas, suggests that reality is like a diamond. As we look through the lens of each prism or facet we can see different aspects of ourselves, of our world, and of the Divine. Or, think of a kaleidoscope. A small turn in any direction gives us a whole new picture. Dreamwork itself provides us with some of these lenses, and sharing our dreams with others allows us to view the images and storylines from yet another lens or prism. Taking our dream exploration out into the world with others can enhance and enlighten our lives.

To further clarify this idea of multifaceted realities of the same scene, here is a waking example. I was sitting in the dappled shade of a large maple tree in a well-manicured garden next to my friend Julie. She commented on a graceful stone arch under the trees, but I couldn't see it at all since I was turned slightly to the right to face her as we talked. What I saw was the whimsical cat sculpture that Julie couldn't see from her vantage point. We were sitting right next to each other on a bench, but that ten-degree angle of difference in perspective made each of us blind to what the other could see. The cat and the arch were both there, but we would have missed seeing one or the other without that second set of eyes. In a similar way, sharing our dreams with others can give us new perspectives such as these.

Dream Circles

One of the ways to share dreams and the joys of their teachings is to start a dream circle of your own. If you recall from the introduction, my friend Eve moved to Boston from New York and began a dream circle here. She asked me and a few other friends to join her in this. I still remember my response, "Sure. What's a dream circle?"

I was at just the right time and place in my life to recognize that this was something I had to say yes to, even before I knew exactly what I was signing up for. One could say that I had an intuitive sense that this was something big for me. Eve explained to me that at its most basic, a dream circle is a group that gets together regularly to share and work on understanding what their dreams mean.

While participating as a member in my own peer-led dream circle, I also began leading dream circles professionally for others. My personal group has no leaders; we all share the group maintenance tasks. In my professional circle I function as the "formal" leader; my job in those groups is to teach dreamwork skills, hold the space, and attend to group dynamics as needed, to maintain a safe space for all participants. I started out leading these circles as twelve-week groups. Over the years, as members kept on renewing their twelve-week commitments, the format changed to an open-ended group with a minimum six-month commitment to ensure group continuity. (As a professional group worker, after teaching group work at Boston University School of Social Work for fifteen years, I know how important group continuity and commitment is.) This group has now been ongoing for more than twenty years. New members have come and gone, some staying a year or two, and some for ten or more.

To start your own dream circle, first know that there is no one right or wrong format. There are several decisions to make at the onset, and then the rest of the structure can evolve as the group does. The first decision is whether or not there will be a formal group leader, a rotating system of leadership, or a peer-based style with no designated leadership. You also need to decide if this is a closed membership group (this means that there are four or six or eight members, and no one else can join once it is full), or an open-ended drop-in group that lets people come and go. It depends on the purpose of the group and the needs and goals of the members. I know of a local group that operates in this drop-in style with four to twelve members at each monthly meeting.

There are pros and cons to each system. If most members are new to dreamwork, and one has significantly more experience, it might make sense to have it led by that member. Otherwise, either a rotating leadership or a leaderless peer group is fine. At the first meeting, you decide how often you want to meet and whether to commit to a certain number of meetings to start with, or an open-ended group. To respect everyone's very busy lives, I would suggest a time-limited group to start with (maybe ten to twelve meetings) if you are planning to meet weekly or biweekly. A monthly group is more feasible if the plan is to meet "indefi-nitely." We want to set it up for success. Trying to set up a weekly long-term group can often be a recipe for failure. Most of us have too many commitments to really show up every week for an extended period of time. Absent members affect the life and the dynamics of the group, as well as those who are present.

Once the nuts and bolts of when, where, and how often to meet are established, the next decision is number of members. Again, there is no right or wrong, just a need for clarity. Options can include:

- Anyone who wants to come can attend as long as they abide by our group rules.

- We cap the group at X number of members and it is then closed to newcomers until someone leaves.

- We recruit four or six members and then close it to newcomers.

Speaking of group rules, again, not many are needed, but a few are essential for the success of the group. The first one is about confidentiality. For members to feel safe enough to share the truths of their deepest selves through dreams, they need to be assured that this information will not go outside the group, show up on social media, or even be shared with family members and friends. A good template for confidentiality is that members are welcome to share their own personal material from their dreams or the work on their dreams, but may not share anyone else's outside the group.

The second important group rule is to abide by the gold standard that the dream belongs to the dreamer. Although we may have associations and insights to offer the dreamer about the meaning of their dream, the final say belongs to them. It may be useful to use Taylor's method of prefacing a comment with, "If this were my dream, I might think that…" This way we are both honoring the integrity of the dreamer and free to have our own learnings and resonance with the material. Decide together how you want to address bringing food or beverages. Kids and teens love to participate in dream circles too, so consider it if you are a scout leader, counselor, teacher, or other professional who works with youngsters. Discussing dreams is a great way to get young people to share deeply without feeling too exposed.

As in any group, conflicts can arise. Do you want to have a plan for how you might deal with this, or will you just see what comes up? Some issues will need to be worked out, and with others you can simply agree to disagree. Issues such as intrusive behavior or serious confidentiality breaches might be deal-breakers or grounds for a warning or an invitation to leave the group.

You might find some of your deepest relationships through the sacred art of dream-sharing. Most important is to have fun in the process, enjoy your own *ahas*, and delight in the joy of discovery in your fellow group members.

The Rest of the Journey Home

Over the course of these pages, we have learned how to remember our dreams and how to invite a dream in through the process of incubation. We discovered that we can engage with the dreamtime in our waking world by paying attention to signs and signals of synchronicity and meaning. When we are mindfully awake to our dreams, we can time travel, cross the threshold to other worlds and planes of knowing, and connect with guides and loved ones to get their advice.

We recognize that dreams come to us with many possible layers of knowledge and wisdom. To fully reap the rich harvest they can bring us, we can use a format such as the PARDES system, which features four layers: simple or surface (the *P'shat* layer), hinted at (the *Remez* layer), deeply pursued (the *Drash* layer), and the mystery (the *Sod* layer). As we engage with the various characters, landscapes, and other rich imagery of our dreams, we learn how to utilize these elements both for our healing and in our creative pursuits. At this point you have acquired a compendium of tools and techniques with which to engage in dreamwork. Some can be used with both dreams and nightmares; some are better suited for one or the other.

The decision of which method to use for any dream is in part determined by the interests and needs of the dreamer, and the skills and tools of the dream guide. Time is a factor too; you may chose a quick or simple method if you are short on time. If you have the luxury of a long stretch, your dreamwork can include the use of multiple methods of exploration. When working in a group, sometimes you may want to make sure that everyone has time to work briefly on a dream, or you may decide to spend a long time exploring a few dreams more deeply, and have just a few members share each meeting. If you are dream-sharing with just one other person, you may want to take turns, or set up a system like "we'll work on your dream for an hour, then on my dream for an hour." If you and your dream-sharing companions are open to trying some of the embodied, roleplaying, or art-making elements of dreamwork, these methods can add additional insights and fullness to your work. Sitting still, working through associations, discerning how they are relevant to your life, and coming up with an action plan to honor them are always fine methods as well.

Journeying On

Dreamwork is a lifelong journey. Whether you are working on dreams on your own or with other people, remember to pay attention to the recurring themes, characters, and landscapes in your dreams. Some recurring images you will greet as old and dear friends. Others you will notice by their absence, for better or worse. Still others will call to you out of the shadows, or from your own shadow self. To make that journey home, to your own home base, notice if your dreamwork is growing in the direction of resolution, toward quieting and soothing the hurt or stuck places in your waking and sleeping lives. If not, consider finding a counselor or therapist who is trained in dreamwork to help guide you on your journey.

Poet John O'Donohue captures the essence of the dream of coming home to your soul in "Morning Offering."

I bless the night that nourished my heart
To set the ghosts of longing free
Into the flow and figure of dream
That went to harvest from the dark…

As we part ways here, I encourage you to nourish your heart and your soul with your dreams. Thank you for joining me on this journey. Dream on. Dream strong. The phrase "Live Strong" has become synonymous with reclaiming one's power or healing. The world needs strong dreamers today more than ever to heal our peoples and our planet. Reconnect with the wisdom of our ancestors and tribes. Dream strong for yourself. Dream for your family. Dream for your tribe. Dream for the whole world. Be the vessel for dreams to come through. Dream while asleep. Dream while awake. Continued your dream healings in your waking life.

May your dreams bring you light and insight and healing and connection and joy. Many blessings to you on your journey, and may your dreams bring you home.

Appendix 1

TIPS FOR REMEMBERING YOUR DREAMS

1. Be prepared. You can't fool your unconscious, so have dream-recording materials right by your bed so your dreaming self knows you are serious.

2. Accept and value every dream or dream fragment; don't dismiss anything as too trivial or too small. Write down even a word or phrase if that's all that comes through. You will be amazed at how much information you can get out of just one word.

3. Pick an unpressured period of time to try to remember (like a vacation or weekend) if there has been a long period of non-remembering. Dreams, like many of us, rarely respond well to pressure.

4. Allow yourself, whenever possible, to waken spontaneously without an alarm clock. My friend Carolyn called her alarm clock her "dream eraser."

5. On waking, lie still and review the dream in your mind before moving. Allow the lingering images of the last scenes to act as a hook to help you recall earlier portions. Don't jump at it too quickly; allow the images to make their own transition from one side of the veil of sleep to the other.

6. Record your dream before doing anything else—even before sitting up, if possible. Of course, if you remember it later in the day, it's never too late to write it down. I seem to have a penchant for remembering in the shower, so I just keep repeating it to myself until I am dry enough to write it down.

7. If you know that you had a dream but can't remember even a bit of it, write the date and the word "dream" in your dream journal.

8. Share the dream out loud with someone to set it orally as well as in writing.

9. Lie down and bring your body back to the same position that you slept in to stimulate positional recall. I find that if I lie down on my favorite sleeping side and curl up, even later in the day, I can often recapture that *felt sense* of the dream in my body, and then the rest of it rolls in.

10. Imagine wrapping yourself in the dream as you would a shawl. Take the edges of your dream and wrap them around you to envelope you back inside it. Feel in your body the sensation of being wrapped up in a cozy shawl of dreams.

You can physically stretch your hands out and "grab" the edges of your dream as you would an imaginary shawl and wrap it around yourself.

11. Write down your immediate thoughts and feelings as you awaken, even if you don't think they came from the dream. They may have emerged from the hypnopompic or hypnagogic zones, the intermediate states between waking and sleeping. Sometimes we catch a dream this way without realizing it. Remember not to interpret at this phase though.

12. Sketch out or draw your dream. A picture can be worth a thousand words. Sometimes we get insight when we can see the dimensions and colors and shapes of our dream images that words alone can't do justice to.

13. Don't censor your dreams. Be a faithful reporter. After all, you are the only person who will be reading them, unless you chose to share them with others. Don't change or alter the order of events, or the feelings, or the events themselves because they are uncomfortable or embarrassing. You will have a chance to work with them later, but for now, "Just the facts, ma'am."

14. Attend to the feelings in your dreams. *Feelings* refers both to our body sensations and to our emotions. We "feel feelings" in our body. Write down the feeling narrative of your dream, as well as the story narrative. (That is, "In the beginning of the dream I felt [ ], and at this part I felt [ ], and at the end I felt [ ].") This somatosensory narrative will be invaluable later when you get to work on them.

15. Finally, practice dream incubation before going to sleep at night.

Appendix II
TECHNIQUES FOR DREAMWORK

1. After you have written down your dream (in the order in which you dreamed it), reread it and take note of any immediate associations, thoughts, or feelings that come through. Don't discount anything and don't edit. Cast a wide net here; you'll sort through it later.

2. Give your dream a title. Don't think about it; let it come from your gut. If you are surprised by it, so much the better—that means that you have begun to tap into your unconscious self. The title will now be one of your major signposts on the yellow brick road to unpacking the dream. One method of dreamwork that I call "Title and Re-Title" includes titling your initial dream, and then after working on it to gain the insights and messages from it, seeing if it wants another title. This new title often reflects the wisdom

gleaned from the dreamwork. This can be a simple and wonderful way to see your progress.

3. Write out the emotional narrative of the dream to go alongside the storyline. Notice both the emotions and any sensations in your body at each part of your dream.

4. Identify the CI in your dream, the Central Image. Do you want to start here, or does your dream ask you to work through it in the chronological order in which you dreamed it?

5. Now go back through your dream with a fine-tooth comb and notice what other associations you have to each part of it. Here you are tapping more deeply into the second layer of dreamwork, the *Remez* or hinted at layer. Notice which of the associations you are making contains an aha for you.

6. Make visual associations. Take a compelling image, write the main word down, and draw the child's version of the sun with rays around it. Next, you (and others if you are working with others) should write down any associations or metaphors related to the word at the end of each spoke. I like to use a different colored pencil for each person who participates; it is then easier to see which ones originated with the dreamer and which ones came from someone else. At the end, the dreamer goes back and circles all the options that somehow seem relevant to their dream, choosing both from their own and those others have written.

7. Look for the connections to your life today—are there any places in the dream that seem related to your life in the last few weeks? Something you've been thinking about, dwelling on, or struggling with?

8. Attend to the *a priori* meaning of the image. Look it up, see what qualities this image has in real life, and assess how they might be relevant to your dream and to your life. Remember that *a priori* literally means "from before," meaning the independent valid meanings or qualities of the image regardless of how it appears in your dream. This often allows you to get to the *Drash* or *Sod* layers—the pursued and mystical layers that you probably won't get to by sheer association.

9. Dreamworker Gayle Delaney developed "the Dream Interview." Tell the dreamer (including yourself), "I am from another planet. I have no idea what an X is (an item or image from the dream). What is an X? What is its purpose? Why is it in your dream? What does it feel like to be an X?" Then restate what the dreamer told you using his or her own words. Now make the bridge to waking life—is there anyone or anything in your waking life that is like that? What does this remind you of in your life?

10. Attend to the metaphors, plays on words, puns, or multiple meanings your dream brings you.

11. Use the Gestalt method of animating every object, including the inanimate ones, in your dream and having them talk to you and to each other. Remember how I animated the toilet and gave it a voice. Listen to what the objects as well as the people have to say in the dream. Using this method, dreamworker Robert Hoss tells us to describe the qualities of this object as if we were describing ourself: our purpose, what we look like as the object, what we do, and what we need. Also ask yourself about this part of yourself,

perhaps even writing out "What is the X part of me? What does the X part of me need or want?"

If you dreamt of a deer hidden in the woods, ask yourself, "What is the deer part of me?" Or combine puns with Gestalt and ask, "What is the dear part of me? What is the dear part of me that is hidden?"

12. Try dream reentry. Instead of working on the dream from the outside in, go inside of the dream and work on it from there. Reenter the dream either at the beginning, or at the point that is calling to you, and then speak/act it out in the first person as if it is actually occurring now. Speak in the first person as you "walk" through the dream.

13. Incorporate active imagination and adding resources. Either from the inside or the outside of the dream, add resources and guides, or make different choices, since you are, in a sense, re-dreaming it present time. This type of reentry, moving around, and possibly adding or changing things is known by the Jungian phrase *active imagination*.

14. Related to both Gestalt and reentry is the Jungian process of amplification. Choose a compelling image and make it bigger, stronger, even more powerful. Let it fill your body and feel it from the inside. If it becomes related to myth, fairy tale, historical figures or eras, a tarot image, a religious text, or the like, it may then become archetypical amplification. This "turns up the volume" on the image to get a better handle on what it means to the dreamer. Jung said amplification allowed us to reach "the tissue that the word or image is embedded in" by means of "analogies, parallels, and active imagination."

15. Re-scripting and Re-ending: Remembering that this is your dream, it came from your psyche, and therefore you can go inside and make any changes you'd like, make a different choice or change the ending. This is an opportunity to have it come out differently in the end, for this is not where the dream needed to end; it is simply where you woke up or stopped remembering it.

16. A picture is worth a thousand words. Sometimes if we draw or paint or sculpt the images from our dreams, we get a whole new perspective on them. 3-D gives us more dimensions than linear or flat or verbal representations.

17. Embodiment and dream theater: Act out your dream or a portion of it. Become all of the characters yourself, or enlist friends and family to do it with you as you play the part of the director. Feel into the parts, let yourself become the boulder, or the river, or the hawk and see what your body wants as it holds this felt sense.

18. Ritual: When we DO something as a result of our dream, we are starting the process of actualizing it in our lives. Inner work often requires a physical act that affirms it. Sometimes we need to make a big change; sometimes a small symbolic one is sufficient to get the ball rolling. Sometimes the smaller rituals are the most powerful. Send an email, or better yet, an actual letter or phone call to the relative you dreamed about. A highly conscious ritual sends a highly powerful message to your unconscious.

19. Notice energy levels in your dream. What is the strongest place in the dream? Are there places in your dream that you shy away from or feel resistance toward? What happens if

you let yourself approach rather than avoid those places? Are there places in the dream where you the dreamer or you the listener feel unable to focus or where you get distracted? What might be the significance of that? Can you let yourself go to these elusive or uncomfortable places?

20. Meditate, pray, or go into a light trance while focused on your dream. These states of being are closer to the state that we are in while dreaming, and they can allow us to retrieve information from other dimensions more easily. When we are very relaxed, we are more receptive to receiving information from deeper parts of ourselves and from the wider universe.

21. Incubate the dream or part of the dream for additional guidance. Before bed on subsequent nights, write in your dream journal your intention to gain more insight or wisdom into the [ ] part of your previous dream, or what symbol [ ] means.

22. Look for the gifts from every dream, including the gifts that may be hidden away inside of the nightmares. What has the dream offered to you, and how will you honor that?

Appendix III
....

USING THE GAIA METHOD
WITH NIGHTMARES

Pre-Dreamwork GAIA Safety Protocol: Stage 1

In keeping with Judith Herman's phase-oriented treatment of trauma, first address the safety needs of the dreamer before going into the dream itself.

1. The dreamer tells you they have a dream. You ask if they want to share it.

2. After they share it, you ask if they want to work on it.

3. Share with the dreamer the knowledge that there is a gift in every dream. Even the scariest nightmare has unpolished gems within. Our goal for doing dreamwork is to find the gift that brings the dreamer greater empowerment and

235

healing. We will orient ourselves in that direction before going on. This is part of the "guided" active imagination approach in which we presuppose that there will be something positive or healing to find out, but do not presuppose what that may be. It might be information, direction, insight, connection, or an object with meaning.

4. At this time, ask for the spontaneous working title of the dream (chances are that it reflects the emotional distress and a negative belief). Ask for the SUDS (subjective unit of distress) on a scale of 0–10, with 0 being no upset or distress, and 10 being the worst upset they can imagine.

5. Ask, "What do you need to feel safe and protected enough to begin to address this dream or to be able to go back inside the dream and find some answers and healing?" Explore options of people the dreamer needs for safety—real or imagined, alive or dead—that they know or knew or just read about. If they need suggestions, you can include yourself as an option, as well as family members, friends, pets, characters from books or movies, sacred or power beings, or familiar objects. Include invitations to God, any sacred being or higher power, Jesus, Buddha, angels, nature spirits, departed relatives, spirit animals, guides, and so on. Use their wording for these powers.

6. Ask next, "What protective objects do you need for potential obstacles you may encounter in the dreamscape?" The idea is to be very specific. Remind them that since this is a dream journey of their own creation, they can bring anyone or anything they want into it. Some examples of safe passage objects have included a flashlight, since it was dark

in the dream; a baseball bat for protection; an invisibility cloak; pets; a blanket, real or imaginary; and a piece of jewelry with special meaning.

7. Get the details—the colors, size, texture, sensations. We are beginning to weave in GAIA methods even as we prepare to work on the dream. You are guiding their exploration, but not interfering in it.

8. Be prepared to keep asking, "Is there anything else you need to be perfectly safe?" and saying, "Check to be sure you are really safe and ready" before reentering the dream. I can't emphasize enough the importance of this preparatory work—it makes the difference between a successful dream reentry or dreamwork, and an experience that could be potentially re-traumatizing. Be cognizant of the difference for the dreamer between "unsafe" and "uncomfortable." Uncomfortable is okay, but unsafe is not. Back off if the dreamer feels unsafe; possibly table the dreamwork completely for a time.

9. Find out how old the dreamer is in the dream, and how old they feel in the dream as they retell it—these may not be the same. Get the protection that the youngest part of you that is present needs.

GAIA Protocol Stage 2: Working Inside the Dream

Only after completing the pre-dream preparation, begin the process of dream reentry by speaking aloud the following guiding prompts:

1. What is the best place to enter this dream?

2. Gather your safety people and objects and tell me when you are ready.

3. Go ahead and enter the dream, and tell me when you are there.

4. Are you ready to continue?

5. What happens first? Next? What do you want to do/say? What do you need to stay safe? Anything else? Are you ready to continue now? (Continue with these types of questions as many times as is needed for the dreamer to experience some resolution).

6. Is there anything else you need to say or do to feel complete with this part? (The guide can offer ideas or suggestions if the dreamer if stuck, being sure to give them the choice of which to accept or discard. This can be framed as, "Would you like to …" or, "What about this option …") Does the dream now have an optimal ending? Are you satisfied with how this is resolved?

7. Is there any place in this dream or dream part where you still feel unsafe or unfinished? Check carefully.

8. Gather up the gifts you received from this dreamwork—the words, the objects, the writings, the knowledge you now have.

9. As you prepare to leave this dreamscape, gather your learnings in a way that serves your highest purpose and is in the service of your growth and healing.

10. When the dreamer is "back" out of the dreamscape, ask several of the following questions:

"How are you now?" "What have you discovered?" "What has changed?" "How do you understand this dream/situation now?" "Is there anything else that feels incomplete or not safe?" "What is the SUDS (the subjective unit of distress) now? Has it diminished?" "Has the title of your dream changed? If so, what is it now? How true is that new title?" "How will you incorporate these learnings into your life today?" Reality test the information with current or past real life experiences for emotional congruence.

Additional Options of Dreamwork with Post-Trauma Dreams:

- Make a connection between the dream material and real life (does this remind you of anything in your life, past or present?)

- Discern between dream symbolism and potential memory bursts (could this have actually happened?)

- Follow the thread of a reoccurring dream or theme, and notice how it changes over time as greater integration and healing occurs.

- "Assign" dream incubation as homework between sessions to resolve a dilemma.

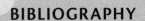

BIBLIOGRAPHY

Aizenstat, Stephen. *Dream Tending: Awakening to the Healing Power of Dreams*. New Orleans, LA: Spring Journal, 2011.

Almaas. A. H. *Facets of Unity: The Enneagram of Holy Ideas*. Berkeley, CA: Diamond Books, 1998.

Amen, Daniel. *Change Your Brain, Change Your Life: The Breakthrough Program for Conquering Anxiety, Depression, Obsessiveness, Lack of Focus, Anger, and Memory Problems*. New York: Three Rivers Press, 1998.

Andrews, Ted. *Animal Speak: The Spiritual & Magical Powers of Creatures Great & Small*. St. Paul, MN: Llewellyn Publications, 2001.

Barasch, Marc Ian. *Healing Dreams: Exploring the Dreams that can Transform Your Life*. New York: Riverhead Books, 2000.

Bosnak, Robert. *A Little Course in Dreams*. Boston, MA: Shambhala Press, 1986.

Bosnak, Robert. *Tracks in the Wilderness of Dreaming: Exploring Interior Landscape through Practical Dreamwork.* New York: Delacorte Press, 1996.

Bulkeley, Kelly. *Dreams of Healing: Transforming Nightmares into Visions of Hope.* New York: Paulist Press, 2003.

Katie, Byron. *Loving What Is: Four Questions that can Change Your Life.* New York: Crown Publishing Co., 2002.

Cartwright, Rosalind. *The Twenty-Four Hour Mind: The Role of Sleep and Dreaming in Our Emotional Lives.* New York: Oxford University Press, 2010.

Carey, Mike. *The Naming of the Beasts.* New York: Orbit, 2009

Conforti, Michael. *Field, Form, and Fate: Patterns in Mind, Nature, and Psyche.* New Orleans, LA: Spring Journal, 2013.

———. Keynote address at the *Journey Conference*, Raleigh, NC. 2012.

Craig, Eric. Presentation at IASD conference, Charlottesville, VA. 1992.

DeBord, J. M. *Dreams 1-2-3: Remember, Interpret and Live Your Dreams.* Charlottesville, VA: Hampton Roads Publishing Co., 2013.

———. *The Dream Interpretation Dictionary: Symbols, Signs, and Meanings.* Canton, MI: Visible Ink Press, 2017.

Delaney, Gayle. *All About Dreams: Everything You Need to Know About Why We Have Them, What They Mean, and How to Put Them to Work for You.* San Francisco: HarperSanFrancisco, 1998.

Deerborn, Carol. "The Spirit of Place." 2012. http://www
.caroldearborn.com/the-spirit-of-place.html.

Estés, Clarissa Pinkola. *Women Who Run With the Wolves: Myths and Stories of the Wild Woman Archetype.* New York: Ballantine Books, 1992.

Frankl, Viktor. *Man's Search for Meaning.* Boston, MA: Beacon Press, 1959.

Frankel, Estelle. *The Wisdom of Not Knowing: Discovering a Life of Wonder by Embracing Uncertainty.* Boulder, CO: Shambhala Publications, 2017.

Frankiel, Tamar, and Judy Greenfeld. *Entering the Temple of Dreams: Jewish Prayers, Movements, and Meditations for the End of the Day.* Woodstock, VT: Jewish Lights Publishing, 2000.

Gendlin, Eugene. *Focusing.* New York: Bantam Books, 1978.

———. *Let Your Body Interpret Your Dreams.* Wilmette, IL: Chiron Publications, 1986.

Golembe, Carla, Painter/Illustrator. www.carlagolembe.com.

Harrisson, Juliette. "The Classical Greek Practice of Dream Incubation and Some Near Eastern Predecessors." Academia. 2009. https://www.academia.edu/277934/The_Classical_Greek_Practice_of_Incubation_and_some_Near_Eastern_Predecessors.

Harner, Michael. *The Way of the Shaman.* San Francisco, CA: HarperOne, 1990.

Hartmann, Ernest. *The Nightmare: The Psychology and Biology of Terrifying Dreams.* New York: Basic Books, 1984.

Hartmann, Ernest, and Robert Kunzendorf. "The Central Image (CI) in Recent Dreams, Dreams that Stand Out, and Earliest Dreams: Relationship to Boundaries." *Imagination, Cognition and Personality* 25, no. 4 (2006): 383–92. https://doi.org/10.2190%2F0Q56-1445-3J16-3831.

———. "Boundaries and Dreams." *Imagination, Cognition and Personality,* 26, no. 1 (2006): 101–15. https://doi.org/10.2190%2FHK76-038K-407M-8670.

Herman, Judith. *Trauma and Recovery.* New York: Basic Books, 1992.

Hobson, Allan. "The New Neuropsychology of Sleep: implications for Psychoanalysis." *Neuro-psychoanalysis: An Interdisciplinary Journal for Psychoanalysis and the Neurosciences,* 1999.

Hoss, Robert. *Dream Language: Self-Understanding Through Imagery and Color.* Ashland, OR: Innersource, 2005.

Houston, Jean. *Jump Time: Shaping Your Future in a World of Radical Change.* Boulder, CO: Sentient Publications, 2004.

IASD, The International Association for the Study of Dreams www.iasd.org: This community-based, vibrant organization brings dreamers together and attends to all aspects of dreaming. It creates online and global dream conferences and provides a wealth of expert dream advice, insight, and information through its member-exclusive *DreamTime* magazine and its academic journal, *Dreaming.*

Janes, Sarah. "A Dream Cure? The Effective Healing Power of Dream Incubation in Ancient Greece." Ancient Origins. Stella Novus. December 15, 2017. https://www

.ancient-origins.net/history-ancient-traditions/dream
-cure-effective-healing-power-dream-incubation-ancient
-greece-009287.

Johnson, Clare R. *Llewellyn's Complete Book of Lucid Dreaming: A Comprehensive Guide to Promote Creativity, Overcome Sleep Disturbances & Enhance Health and Wellness.* Woodbury, MN: Llewellyn Publications, 2017.

Judith, Anodea. *Eastern Body, Western Mind: Psychology and the Chakra System as a Path to the Self.* Berkeley, CA: Celestial Arts, 2004.

Jung, C. G. *Memories, Dreams, and Reflections.* Recorded and edited by Aniela Jaffé. Translated by Richard and Clara Winston. New York: Random House, 1961.

———. *Jung on Active Imagination.* Edited by Joan Chodorow. Princeton, NJ: Princeton University Press, 1997.

———. *Synchronicity: An Acausal Connecting Principle.* London: Routledge, 1985.

Kabat-Zinn, Jon. *Full Catastrophe Living: Using the Wisdom of Your Body and Mind to Face Stress, Pain and Illness.* New York: Bantam Books, 2013.

Kahn, David. Harvard University. Conference presentation at IASD international conference and personal interview. June 2018.

Levoy, Gregg. *Callings: Finding and Following an Authentic Life* and *Vital Signs: The Nature and Nurture of Passion.* New York: Three Rivers Press, 1998.

Malcolm, Lynne, and Olivia Willis. "Songlines: The Indigenous Memory Code." All in the Mind. July 8, 2015. https://

www.abc.net.au/radionational/programs/allinthemind/
songlines-indigenous-memory-code/7581788.

McEwen, Christian. *World Enough & Time: On Creativity and Slowing Down.* Peterborough, NH: Bauhan Publishing, 2011.

McNamara, Patrick. Boston Globe, Boston University School of Medicine. February 3, 2014.

McTaggart, Lynne. *The Field: The Quest for the Secret Force of the Universe.* London: HarperCollins, 2001.

Moore, Thomas. "Why Thomas Moore Believes We're in the Midst of a Religious Revolution," interview by Oprah Winfrey, *SuperSoul Sunday, OWN.* October 18, 2015. https://www.youtube.com/watch?v=lPxEPKrvJpg.

Moss, Robert. *Conscious Dreaming: A Spiritual Path for Everyday Life.* New York: Three Rivers Press, 1996.

———. *The Three Only Things: Tapping the Power of Dreams, Coincidence, & Imagination.* Novato, CA: New World Library, 2007.

Naiman, Rubin. *Healing Night: The Science and Spirit of Sleeping, Dreaming, and Awakening.* Tuscon, AZ: NewMoon Media, 2006.

Neilson, Susie. "We're in a 'Dream Deprivation' Epidemic." The Science of Us. October 17, 2017. https://www.thecut.com/2017/10/were-in-a-dream-deprivation-epidemic.html.

Andrillon, Thomas, Yuval Nir, Chiara Cirelli, Giulio Tononi, and Itzhak Fried. "Single-Neuron Activity and Eye Movements During Human REM Sleep and Awake Vision."

Nature Communications 6, no. 7885 (2015). https://doi
.org/10.1038/ncomms8884.

Oliver, Mary. *New and Selected Poems, Volume One.* Boston,
MA: Beacon Press, 1992.

———. *Thirst.* Boston, MA: Beacon Press, 2009.

O'Donohue, John. *To Bless the Space Between Us: A Book of
Blessings.* New York: Doubleday, 2008.

Patton, Kimberly. "Dream Incubation: Theology and Topography." Dreamtime 19:4, IASD. 2002

Rabinowe, Victoria. "Art and Dreams." Dreamtime, IASD.
Winter 2006.

Rogers, Katharine M. *L. Frank Baum: Creator of Oz: A Biogra-
phy.* New York: St. Martin's Press, 2002.

Schiller, Linda Yael. "Title and Re-Titling the Dream: A Dreamworker's Parallel to EMDR, a Transformational Therapy."
Dreamtime, IASD. Spring 2014.

———. "Getting Unstuck: Using the GAIA Method of Dreamwork to Heal from Trauma." Dreamtime, IASD. Winter
2012.

———. *Dreamwork through the Lens of Kabbalah,* audiotape
from IASD conference presentation, 2007.

———. *Dreamwork and Psychotherapy,* audiotape for
"HomeEd." Massachusetts chapter of the National Association of Social Workers, 2000.

———. "A Song of Grief." In *Send My Roots Rain: A Companion on the Grief Journey*, edited by Kim Langley. Brewster,
MA: Paraclete Press, 2019.

Siegel, Alan. *Dream Wisdom: Uncovering Life's Answers in Your Dreams.* Berkeley, CA: Celestial Arts, 2002.

Stickgold, Robert. Harvard University, conference presentation at IASD international conference. June 2018.

Taylor, Jeremy. *Where People Fly and Water Runs Uphill: Using Dreams to Tap the Wisdom of the Unconscious.* New York: Warner Books, 1992.

Taylor, Jeremy. *The Wisdom of Your Dreams.* New York: Tarcher Penguin, 2009.

Teilhard de Chardin, Pierre. *The Phenomenon of Man.* Translated by Bernard Wall. New York: Harper, 1959.

Nhat Hanh, Thich. Mindfulness and Psychotherapy conference, Boston, MA. November 2017.

Ullman, Rabbi Alan. Personal interview. 2015.

Van de Castle, Robert. *Our Dreaming Mind.* New York: Random House, 1994.

Von Franz, Marie-Louise. *On Dreams and Death.* 1997. Audiotape.

Waggoner, Robert. *The Lucid Dreaming Pack: Gateway to the Inner Self.* New York: Chartwell Books, 2016.

Walker, Matthew. *Why We Sleep: Unlocking the Power of Sleep and Dreams.* New York: Simon and Schuster, 2017.

Wamsley, Erin. "Dreaming, Waking Conscious Experience, and the Resting Brain: Report of Subjective Experience as a Tool in Cognitive Neurosciences." *Frontiers in Psychology* 4, no. 637 (September 2013). https://doi.org/10.3389/fpsyg.2013.00637.

To Write to the Author

If you wish to contact the author or would like more information about this book, please write to the author in care of Llewellyn Worldwide Ltd. and we will forward your request. Both the author and publisher appreciate hearing from you and learning of your enjoyment of this book and how it has helped you. Llewellyn Worldwide Ltd. cannot guarantee that every letter written to the author can be answered, but all will be forwarded. Please write to:

Linda Yael Schiller
℅ Llewellyn Worldwide
2143 Wooddale Drive
Woodbury, MN 55125-2989

Please enclose a self-addressed stamped envelope for reply,
or $1.00 to cover costs. If outside the U.S.A., enclose
an international postal reply coupon.

Many of Llewellyn's authors have websites with additional information and resources. For more information, please visit our website at http://www.llewellyn.com.